SPIES IN THE SKY

WORLD ESPIONAGE

◆◆◆◆◆◆◆◆◆◆◆◆◆

SPIES IN THE SKY

Graham Yost

Facts On File
New York • Oxford • Sydney

Facts On File, Inc.		Facts On File Limited
460 Park Avenue South	or	Collins Street
New York, NY 10016		Oxford OX4 1XJ
USA		United Kingdom

Library of Congress Cataloging-in-Publication Data

Yost, Graham
    Spies in the sky / Graham Yost.
      p. cm. — (World espionage series)
    Bibliography: p.
    Includes index.
    Summary: Follows the history of spy satellites and military satellites and describes how they are used.
    ISBN 0-8160-1942-8
    1. Space surveillance—Juvenile literature. [1. Space surveillance.] I. Title. II. Series: Yost, Graham. World espionage series.
    UG1520.Y67 1989
    623'.71—dc20   89-1385

British CIP data available on request from Facts On File.

Facts On File books are available at special discounts when purchased in bulk quantities for businesses, associations, institutions or sales promotion. Please contact the Special Sales Department of our New York office at 212/683-2244 (dial 800/322-8755 except in NY, AK or HI).

Jacket design by Catherine R. Hyman
Composition by Facts On File, Inc.
Manufactured by R. R. Donnelley & Sons

Printed in the United States of America
10 9 8 7 6 5 4 3 2 1

This book is printed on acid-free paper.

CONTENTS

PREFACE: SETTING THE SCENE

Why do countries spy on one another? To find out what the other side is up to, and through that knowledge to gain an advantage. Over a thousand years ago, Chinese philosopher Sun Tzu, in *The Art of War*, emphasized that good spies gathering good intelligence could make the difference between winning and losing a war.

For a long time, spying was used only during time of war—Genghis Khan was a particularly strong advocate, cleverly sending spies on ahead of him as his Mongol hordes swept across Asia in the 13th century. Throughout the Middle Ages, however, the idea of spying during peacetime began to take shape. Governments realized that finding out what another country was up to *before* war broke out could also prove decisive. By the time the 20th century rolled around, most European powers had some kind of spy service in place.

The United States, however, did not follow the European example. America, with its emphasis on liberty and its abhorrence for government snooping in people's affairs, didn't have such a service for a long time. There was a code-breaking office in the 1920s called The Black Chamber (its most notable success was in breaking the diplomatic codes of the Japanese), but it didn't last long. The secretary of state at the time, Henry Stimson, shut it down, saying, "Gentlemen don't read other people's mail." It wasn't until World War II that America developed a full-fledged spy service, and only then because the United States was about to enter a war.

World War II began in September 1939, when German troops invaded Poland. Germany was then led by Adolf Hitler, head of the fascist Nazi Party, a gang that sought to impose its iron-handed dictatorship over the rest of the world, exterminating all, especially Jews and others it didn't like, in its path. America entered the war in December 1941 when Japan, an ally of Germany's, launched a surprise attack on the American naval base at Pearl Harbor in Hawaii.

Although that attack dealt a devastating blow, the government of President Franklin Delano Roosevelt knew that the United States would eventually enter the war and had been preparing for it. As part of the preparations, Roosevelt had formed the Office of Strategic Services—the OSS—America's first spy service. The OSS performed brilliantly during the war, but after the war it was disbanded. The public and the government felt it had fulfilled its purpose, and there were fears that a spy agency during peacetime might turn into something like Germany's dreaded secret police, the Gestapo. By 1947, however, it became clear that the United States needed an agency to gather foreign intelligence, for it now had a new opponent, a new enemy; a country that a few scant years before had been its ally in defeating Hitler—the Soviet Union.

The United States and the Soviet Union are directly opposed in terms of philosophy of government. In the United States, the founding principles were democracy, liberty and capitalism. Citizens vote for those who will run the government, the government is constitutionally limited in its involvement in people's affairs and there is little regulation of the economy, with an emphasis on self-reliance. The Soviet Union, created by a revolution in 1917, was founded on the principles of communism and totalitarianism—there are no workers and bosses, everyone shares equally in the country's wealth, and the government directly controls nearly every aspect of a person's life.

In 1945 America dropped the first atomic bomb. By the end of the decade the Soviet Union had developed its own nuclear weapons. Now the contest between these two ideologically opposed nations took on very high stakes. It became imperative for both sides to know what the other side was up to. The Soviet Union already had its spy service (then called the NKVD, and now known as the KGB), and in 1947 the United States created its own peacetime spy group, the Central Intelligence Agency (CIA).

The Soviets had an easier job of spying on the United States than the United States did spying on the Soviet Union. It was and still is easy to get foreign agents into America but almost impossible to get them into Russia, with its close surveillance of its own population. This book is primarily about the efforts made by the United States to find out what was going on behind the closed Russian borders. The American spy-masters realized that if they couldn't get agents into Russia on the ground, then maybe they could take a look down from above. What they needed were spies in the sky.

INTRODUCTION: THE PERFECT SPY

The perfect spy would be on duty 24 hours a day, every day of the year, in all kinds of weather, without so much as a peep of discontent. This perfect spy would tell you the whereabouts of every missile, every tank and every enemy soldier. This perfect spy would be virtually untouchable by the enemy. This perfect spy wouldn't have to be "handled"—wouldn't have to be stroked, cajoled or coerced into spying—and would never switch allegiance and defect to the other side. The perfect spy would be better than James Bond. For one thing, this spy wouldn't even need to use a gun to get the job done, and for another, it wouldn't waste time romancing foreign agents with expensive champagne.

The perfect spy does exist. It weighs more than 30,000 pounds and is about the size of a railroad boxcar. And, it doesn't come cheap; it costs well over $100 million. This perfect spy is the United States' KH-12 spy satellite, now orbiting the Earth at an altitude of 100 miles or more. Incredibly, from that distance, this perfect spy can see things the size of a deck of playing cards.

Of course, the KH-12 is not much interested in playing cards. It's up there to monitor the Soviet deployment of SS-20 nuclear missiles, and to observe Chinese troop movement along the Vietnamese border, among other things.

Most people in the United States don't know about the KH-12. They may have heard about spy satellites that can read license plates from space (they can't really)—but they don't know anything specific. That's primarily because, officially, there is no such thing as a KH-12 and no such thing as a spy satellite program. While the job of the spy satellite is to uncover the secrets of other nations, it is the nature of the spy satellite itself that it is one of America's closest kept secrets. Indeed, until the early 1980s, many U.S. senators and congressmen didn't know that the National Reconnaissance Office (NRO)—a section of the Air Force Intelligence created in 1960 to oversee the spy satellite program—even existed, although it gobbled up nearly $3 billion of taxpayers' money every year.

The spy satellite program constitutes a second U.S. space program. We all know about what NASA has done in space—the Apollo program that put men on the Moon, and the shuttle program that built and operated the world's first reusable spacecraft. But we don't all know about what the U.S. Air Force and the Central Intelligence Agency have done in space—from Discoverer and SAMOS, the first spy satellites, to the KH-11 and KH-12 of today. We all know that NASA has spent tens of billions of dollars on programs over the past 30 years, but we don't all know that the NRO, the CIA and others involved in the spy satellite program have, over the same period, probably spent more than $100 billion.

We don't know about it because it is a *black* program. In intelligence parlance, a *white* program is something that the public is allowed to know everything about, such as the Apollo missions. Black programs are conducted in the shadows, outside of the public eye. The space shuttle is considered a gray program. It appears to be white but it has some black mixed in: those military flights with "unidentified payloads." The spy satellite program, though, is really beyond black. It is so hidden and surrounded with such secrecy that it is, in the words of author William E. Burrows, "deep black."

It is hard to believe that something larger than the Apollo and space shuttle programs has gone on without the public knowing it, and that over *$100 billion* have been spent without any public accounting. However, that is the case, and it will continue to be the case, for spy satellites have become indispensable to the security of the United States. On March 15, 1967, in a speech to a small gathering in Nashville, Tennessee, President Lyndon Johnson made a supposedly off-the-record remark about the spy satellite program: "I wouldn't want to be quoted on this, but we've spent $35 to 40 billion on the space program [that included the NASA "white" programs]. And if nothing else had come out of it except the knowledge we've gained from space photography, it would be worth 10 times what the whole program has cost. Because, tonight, we know how many missiles the enemy has."

1

GAINING THE HIGH GROUND

Military commanders throughout history have always sought to seize the high ground in battle. Being on top of the hill has always been superior to being at the bottom. To a degree it's a matter of gravity—shooting down at an enemy is easier than shooting up at him. But there's more to it than that. It's also easier to spy down on your enemy from above than it is to spy up at him.

In *The Art of War*, ancient Chinese scholar Sun Tzu wrote of the importance of spying, of finding out in advance what one's opponent is doing. For most of history this has meant sending spies into an opponent's camp to secure secrets. But it has also involved using the high ground to get a look, from a distance, at the preparations the enemy is making.

There were undoubtedly times in prehistory when members of warring tribes would try to gain the upper hand by climbing trees to look down at the enemy village. In ancient battles, battle towers were carried into the fray and used as observation posts. But trees and battle towers can only go so high. The dream, even then, was to get a bird's-eye view by leaving the ground entirely.

The first record of trying to spy this way appears in ancient Chinese and Japanese folklore where observers—no doubt terrified—were strapped to huge kites and hoisted into the wind to view distant enemy emplacements.

1

BALLOONS

The first true forerunner of the spy plane and spy satellite was the hot air balloon, the 18th-century invention of the Montgolfier brothers of France. It was not long before the military recognized its potential and pressed it into service. Napoleon's army made some use of balloons for spying. Napoleon even took a balloon brigade with him on his campaign to Egypt. One of the first to think of photographing the field of battle from a balloon was Gaspard Felix Tourchon, a staunch advocate of balloon reconnaissance. In 1858 he became the first to photograph from a balloon and he thought the possibilities were astounding. He equated the balloon with a village belfry from which the officers of the general staff could make observations, but noted that he could position his belfry anywhere, and with photographic apparatus, would be able to send intelligence photographs to the general staff every 15 minutes.

Tourchon's enthusiasm notwithstanding, the balloon's use for spying didn't really catch on until the American Civil War in the 1860s. Key figures in American ballooning at this time—John Wise, John La Mountain and Thaddeus Lowe—all worked for the Union army.

Wise and his son built their first balloon entirely out of silk, and they outfitted it specifically for war with metal plating across the bottom of the basket to ward off bullets. Balloons used for this purpose were tethered: They were connected to the ground by a long line, thus limiting the view of the observers who rode in the baskets.

La Mountain, curious as to what the enemy was doing over the horizon, audaciously cut his tether so he could float freely over enemy-held territory. He refined his technique and devised a method for his daring: He would drift low over the enemy, then dump ballast and rise up fast into the prevailing winds that he hoped would take him back home. This worked—to a degree—but was still somewhat haphazard and dangerous. La Mountain didn't know if he would drift over anything of interest or just sail past forest and farm fields. And if he did pass over the heads of the Confederates he was sure to draw a hail of gun and cannon fire.

Wise and La Mountain, for the most part, could be characterized as adventurers, while Thaddeus Lowe brought a measure of scientific rigor to the arena of military ballooning. Lowe took up ballooning for scientific research and only saw the military applications one day when his balloon accidentally drifted over Confederate territory. In an effort to convince the Union army of the usefulness of balloons, he arranged for a personal demonstration for President Abraham Lincoln. The president was impressed and gave Lowe his support. Lowe is credited with such innovations as devising a calcium light that could be used to take nighttime aerial photographs, phosphorescent signal balloons and an advanced photographic enlarger.

But balloons never caught on entirely with the military, and after the Civil War they generally fell into disuse for reconnaissance. For one thing, when tethered, balloons afforded a limited view, and when floating freely, their course was unpredictable. And they made an excellent target for the enemy.

Early in the 20th century, Alfred Maul, an engineer in Dresden, Germany, proposed a radical idea for taking photographs from the air—the use of rockets. In 1904 he began to experiment with sending cameras up in small rockets. By 1912 he had developed a gyro-stabilized system that delivered good, clear photographs. Dresden was also the site of another, somewhat humorous, development in aerial photography. On sale at a Dresden photographic fair in 1909 were photographs taken by tiny cameras strapped to the bellies of homing pigeons.

But neither Maul's rockets nor the pigeon photographers rose to prominence in the field of aerial reconnaissance. In that first decade of the 20th century there was another new invention that left balloons, rockets and pigeons far behind—the airplane.

THE FIRST SPY PLANES

While now we think of fighters and bombers as being true military planes, the first military use of the airplane was for reconnaissance. The idea of the fighter plane was only developed as a defense for the vulnerable planes sent in on reconnaissance missions. Dogfights would occur between these escort planes and the enemy planes sent up to shoot down the spies.

In the beginning of spy plane photography, aerial photographs were taken with a camera that the photographer—often the pilot—maneuvered out over the edge of the airplane. As technology improved, the photographer no longer had to risk his life by leaning precariously out the side of the cockpit. Cameras were mounted on the sides of the planes or over holes cut in the floor of the aircraft. The cameras were also set on rubber pads to absorb the vibration caused by the engine and the motion, which would blur the images. Pictures were taken both vertically (straight down) and obliquely (to the side).

Tethered balloons and dirigibles (like the Goodyear blimp seen over football and baseball games today) were also used for reconnaissance during World War I, but as in the Civil War, they proved to be large, easy targets, and were often ripped to shreds by enemy fire.

After World War I ended, the United States relaxed its military stance and research into aerial reconnaissance dropped off, as did research and development in other military areas. But some knew that war would again loom on the horizon and they continued to promote research. In the field of aerial reconnaissance, the man who kept research and development alive was George W. Goddard.

Goddard strove to improve the ground resolution of photographs—that is, the degree of detail on the ground that can be seen in a photograph taken from high in the air. One of the determining factors in a camera's resolution is its focal length, the distance from the camera lens to the point where the image focuses. So, Goddard built huge, long-focal-length cameras.

Goddard also developed the first nighttime aerial photography. His system seems archaic now, but it worked. He towed a glider, packed with explosives and bright flare material, behind a reconnaissance plane, and then detonated the glider, illuminating the ground below as he opened the camera's shutter. His first nighttime photograph was of Rochester, New York, on November 20, 1925.

Another Goddard achievement was the strip camera. At that time photographs taken out of the sides of planes flying on low-altitude reconnaissance missions were blurred by the motion. Flying as low as 25 feet in order to see beneath camouflage coverings, pilots called these "dicing missions" because they felt like they were gambling with the devil. Goddard found the answer to the problem of blurred photographs at a horse track in California.

At the finish, the track employed a shutterless camera to capture a clean picture of the horses as they crossed the line. Instead of a shutter, the camera had an open slit, and the film was pulled across the slit, moving at the same speed as the horses, producing one long, frozen, unblurred picture. Goddard employed this principle in his aerial cameras, with the film set to move backwards over the camera slit at the same speed as the plane was moving forward over the ground. This principle is illustrated by how someone walking down an up escalator can stay in the same spot.

Other Goddard achievements included early infrared film (which can record light below the visible spectrum) and color film. He also pioneered the use of two lenses for stereo pictures. With two pictures of the same feature—a gun emplacement, perhaps—laid side by side and viewed together through a stereoscope (which focuses one eye on one picture and the other on the other picture), the brain is tricked into thinking it is seeing in three dimensions.

Goddard also demonstrated how quickly aerial pictures could be delivered to analysts. One day in 1927 he took aerial photographs of Fort Leavenworth prison, developed the photos in the air and then, using the then-new technology of radio photo transmission, sent the photos through the air to New York. This was *near-real time* reconnaissance photography. Getting images to analysts almost as the events are occurring remains a major goal for spies in the sky, one that is only now just being reached.

Another Goddard of the period also made some major contributions to the advancement of high-flying photography. He was Dr. Robert Goddard, often considered the father of American rocket science. His pioneering work with liquid-fueled rockets in the 1920s helped lay the groundwork for the space and missile age of the 1950s and 1960s. On July 17, 1929, he sent up a camera in a liquid-fueled rocket. In truth, though, Goddard wasn't thinking of reconnaissance or of launching rockets into space. He was most interested in the use of cameras in atmospheric research.

Perhaps the most interesting photo reconnaissance booster of the period was an Australian, Sidney Cotton. Like many others in the late 1930s, Cotton saw war between England and Germany as inevitable. He knew that as war approached, accurate maps and aerial photographs of Europe would be invaluable. But the full potential of photo reconnaissance was still not entirely appreciated by military planners. To them it was only valuable tactically, in the heat of actual battle, and doing reconnaissance and mapping ahead of time didn't seem worth the effort. Cotton ignored them and went ahead on his own.

Cotton set up an operation in London in 1939 as war rapidly approached. He established a fake, cover business that would give him reason to travel all over Europe in his private plane. These business trips were really just reconnaissance missions, and Cotton took thousands of pictures as he crisscrossed the continent, often "accidentally" straying off course. He took pictures of airfields, railroads, bridges, army headquarters, oil fields and the like. British military planners were astounded by what Cotton had accomplished. In fact, they were so impressed that in mid-1940 the RAF (Royal Air Force) took over Cotton's operation—and let Cotton go!

During World War II many of the advances in photo reconnaissance were simply improvements on the work George Goddard had done in the 1920s and 1930s—with further development of infrared film, greater use of color film, as well as stereoscopic images. Eastman Kodak produced higher quality film that would make images less grainy, therefore affording higher resolution. And, bigger and better cameras were built, in particularly a series by Dr. James Baker, an astronomer and optics expert from Harvard University. Baker's cameras were huge, with focal lengths ranging from five feet, all the way up to a truly astounding 20 feet.

Perhaps the greatest advance during the war, however, came not in the field of technology of cameras and film, but in the field of photo analysis, the art of figuring out just what has been captured on film.

PRINCIPLES OF PHOTO INTERPRETATION

When it is reported that a KH-12 spy satellite can pick out things as small as a pack of playing cards from 100 miles away, it doesn't mean that one can look at a KH-12 photograph and say, "There's a pack of playing cards." It does mean that something that small would appear as a speck, distinguishable from the background. Deciding that it is indeed a pack of playing cards would be the job of the photo interpreter, or PI.

In the Cuban missile crisis in the fall of 1962, when the Soviet Union began placing nuclear missiles in Cuba, President John Kennedy and his advisers had to trust the PIs when they said that the little lines and shapes on the pictures taken from spy planes flying over Cuba really were missile tents and launchers and warhead storage bunkers. To Kennedy and his men, they were just lines and shapes.

To the PI, however, such lines and shapes tell a story. By World War II, there had passed more than 20 years of aerial photography and a certain amount of basic PI knowledge had been amassed. By this time PIs knew what a rail line looked like from the air as opposed to a road; the rail line is narrower, with longer straights and broader curves. And they knew what military installations looked like as well. In an interview, former American PI Dino Brugioni put it this way:

> If I see a strict pattern, then a flag goes up. That's the sign of the military. Everything will be evenly spaced. They won't put one gun battery here, the next 33 feet along, and then the other after that 57 feet further. They'll all be 60 feet, or whatever, from each other.

A major development in photo interpretation during the war was specialization. PIs specialized in one particular area that would be photographed from the air again and again. It might be one airfield or one tank factory. By looking at successive photographs, that PI could tell if anything had changed. One British PI, Constance Babbington-Smith, specialized in photos of Germany's rocket test facility located on the Baltic, at Peenemunde. On one photograph she saw "something I did not understand—unlike anything I had seen before...A tiny cruciform shape, set exactly on the lower end of...inclined rails—a midget aircraft actually in position for launching." That was the first direct evidence of Germany's "buzz bomb," the V-1 rocket that would soon terrorize Britain.

Other PIs specialized in types of installations—they would recognize German antiaircraft batteries or tank shapes, for the regularity in shapes that Dino Brugioni looked for is pervasive in the military. For example, if the Germans built an antiaircraft battery one way outside of Dresden, they would likely build it exactly the same way outside of Frankfurt. PIs and others who specialized in rail lines, airfields or factories would then be brought in to consult on other photographs, to help other PIs determine what their pictures contained.

A DANGEROUS MISSION

Reconnaissance flying continued to be exceptionally dangerous throughout the war. Reconnaissance planes had to fly at a relatively low altitude, below the clouds, to get the pictures they needed. Perhaps the most famous reconnaissance pilot of the war was French aviator Antoine de Saint-Exupery, also known as the author of the children's classic *The Little Prince*. In *Flight to Arras* he described this particular hell—flying low:

> I am flying now at two thousand three hundred feet beneath a ceiling of heavy clouds. If I were to rise a mere hundred feet Dutertre [the photographer] would be blind. Thus we are forced to remain visible to the anti-aircraft batteries and play the part of the archer's target for the Germans. Two thousand feet is a forbidden altitude. Your machine serves as a mark for the whole plain. You drain the cannonade of a whole army. You are within range of every caliber. You dwell an eternity in the field of fire of each successive weapon. You are not shot at with cannon but beaten with a stick. It is as if a thousand sticks were used to bring down a single walnut.

And there was another problem—reconnaissance planes were completely defenseless. They were stripped of guns partly to make the planes lighter in order to fly faster, but also so that the pilot would not go on attack, which could ruin the photographic mission. The planes were utterly vulnerable, not only to fire from below, but also to attack from fighter planes from above. To Saint-Exupery, this was the greatest fear.

> The fighters come down on you like lightning. Having spotted you from fifteen hundred feet above, they take their time. They weave, they orient themselves, take careful aim. You know nothing of this. You are the mouse lying in the shadow of the bird of prey. The mouse fancies that it is alive. It goes on frisking in the wheat.

But it is already the prisoner of the retina of the hawk, glued tighter to that retina than to any glue, for the hawk will never leave it now.

And thus you, continuing to pilot, to daydream, to scan the earth, have already been flung outside the dimension of time because of a tiny black dot on the retina of a man.

Not long after dawn on the morning of July 31, 1944, Saint-Exupery took off on a reconnaissance flight from Corsica, bound for the mountains. He never came back.

The information that these reconnaissance missions brought back was invaluable. One of the most important things learned was that Sidney Cotton had been right. Reconnaissance photography should be undertaken in times of peace just in case there is a war. This realization came when military planners discovered that their maps were inaccurate or years out of date.

Thus developed the concept of strategic reconnaissance. Instead of just photographing things of immediate, tactical interest—for example, rail lines and airfields—there would also be a need for reconnaissance with longer-term goals, such as determining the state of the enemy's uranium mining capabilities. This meant that reconnaissance should be conducted during peacetime, and that, too, posed a radical concept. By 1945, however, with the Germans and Japanese in retreat, American politicians and military planners identified the next enemy, a country that was at that time still any ally—the Soviet Union. The United States realized, even before the end of World War II, that reconnaissance of the Soviet Union would be a good idea. The question was: How?

2
THE U-2

The United States and the Soviet Union have been at each other's throats for a long time now.

In 1917 a revolution in Russia brought the communists, led by V. I. Lenin, into power. Communism is a system devised by 19th-century social critic and historian Karl Marx and his collaborator, Friedrich Engels. The goal of communism is to create a classless society—one with no workers and no bosses—where everyone shares in the labor and shares in the rewards. The twist Lenin and his followers, the Bolsheviks, added was that this society should be ruled by one party—the Communist Party. In practice, the new Russia, the Union of Soviet Socialist Republics, became a totalitarian state, where the one party, through the various apparata of government (including a ruthless secret police) controlled every aspect of Soviet life.

The United States has been the enemy of the Soviet Union since 1917 (for a long time Soviet citizens were taught to think of the United States as "Enemy Number One"). In the 1920s and 1930s, direct conflict between the two countries was limited. It was a matter of opposing ideologies: communism vs. capitalism, totalitarianism vs. democracy. However, the opponents never came to blows. And in World War II, these ideological opponents actually became allies, united against the common foe of Adolf Hitler's Nazi Germany.

World War II changed both countries, however. Before the war, both the United States and the Soviet Union had been isolationists to a degree. However, the war thrust them both to the forefront of world affairs. Before the war ended, even as those two countries were still allies, many realized that the conflict between the United States and the U.S.S.R. would dominate world affairs for the foreseeable future.

The United States took the lead in possessing the world's first nuclear weapons (indeed there were even some military planners in the United States who suggested that America should have used that advantage and bombed Russia before it built its own bomb). The Soviets detonated their first atomic bomb in 1949. At that point both countries were nuclear powers, and they were both expanding their rival influences around the world as fast as possible. They were two opposing *superpowers* and they were sworn enemies.

All countries believe it is essential to spy on their enemies, and the United States is no exception. Urgently needing to find out what was happening inside the Soviet Union, the United States faced a major obstacle—the totalitarian nature of Soviet society. While the Soviets infiltrated hundreds of spies into the United States, it was almost impossible for the United States to send spies into Russia. The Soviet Union is a closed society. The government monitors everything its citizens are doing at all times. Everyone must carry identity papers, which may be checked several times throughout the day, and informers are everywhere. The few spies the United States did have in Russia were, for the most part, Soviet citizens who agreed to spy for the West. There weren't enough of them to gather the amount of intelligence that America required.

One option was simply to fly over the Soviet Union and take pictures by conducting strategic reconnaissance. Reconnaissance flights probably began even before the war ended. The spy workhorse of the period was the RB-47, which was basically the successful Boeing B-47 turbojet bomber adapted for reconnaissance missions (which is why it was the *RB*-47). This plane was jammed with equipment designed to gather both PHOTINT (PHOTographic INTelligence) and ELINT (ELectronic INTelligence— such as radar signals). However, the RB-47 was the size of a bomber and had a flight ceiling of 40,000 feet, which made it an excellent target for Soviet antiaircraft gunners. It was really only good for short duration border penetration. It would dash into Soviet airspace, trigger radar alerts for the ELINT crews on board to monitor, take pictures of anything near the border and dash back out again before it was shot down.

The United States also used modified F-86 Sabrejet fighters (RF-86s) for higher-speed photo recon work. These planes could streak in farther over Soviet territory and were harder to shoot down (not that the Soviets didn't try to shoot them down, and not that they didn't succeed sometimes). On many of these dangerous missions the Sabrejets were accompanied by fighters to ward off attack. On January 22, 1954, a dogfight took place over the Yellow Sea between Sabrejet fighter escorts and Soviet MiGs. The American downed one MiG and escaped unscathed. Other times they were not so lucky. By the end of the 1940s, the Soviets had shot down 40 reconnaissance planes.

Not only were these missions dangerous, they also were not bringing back the desired intelligence. The Central Intelligence Agency wanted pictures of what was going on deep behind the Soviet borders. These areas in the middle of the country were out of reach of the RB-47s and RF-86s. The CIA needed a plane that could fly high and fast enough to avoid being shot down.

Until that time, all reconnaissance planes were modified bombers or fighters. During the war, however, a program was instituted to build a plane just for reconnaissance—the F-12. The plane would fly at 470 mph, at a height of 49,000 feet. Before it was ready to go into action, however, the Soviets brought a new fighter into service that could have brought the F-12 down, and so the program was canceled.

The CIA desperately wanted pictures of the Kapustin Yar missile test facility. Unfortunately, it was situated far behind the border. The CIA asked the Air Force to send one of their planes over the Soviet Union to get the pictures. This would be an overflight—flying right across the country, not just looping in and out over the border. The Air Force quite sanely refused.

So, the CIA turned to friends in the RAF in Britain and asked if they'd do it. Up to the challenge, the RAF agreed. They regretted the decision. It was a hell of a flight. The plane flew from West Germany, right across the Soviet Union, and landed in Iran. It was hounded the entire way by antiaircraft fire and pursued by Soviet fighters. It picked up photos of Kapustin Yar, but it also picked up a slew of bullet holes. The CIA, however, was most pleased with the results and asked the RAF when they could fly again. The RAF said never.

Another series of attempts to get pictures of the hidden territories deep within the Soviet Union didn't involve planes—they involved balloons. This was reminiscent of John La Mountain's and Thaddeus Lowe's free-flying exploits over Confederate territory in the Civil War. Huge, unmanned balloons, loaded down with cameras, were launched from Western Europe in the hope that prevailing winds would carry them across the Soviet Union to the Sea of Japan, where they could be recovered. Most of these balloons were never seen again. Several were shot down by the Soviets, who used them to great propaganda advantage. The few that were recovered by the United States returned only a small number of photographs of intelligence value. This was because there was no way to direct the balloons over anything of interest, and they were more likely to photograph farm fields and forests than missile test sites.

The need to find out what the Soviets were up to behind their borders became ever more urgent in the early 1950s. The United States had been operating from a position of confident military superiority since the end of the war.

Although the Soviets had developed their first atom bomb years before the Americans thought they would, by 1954 the United States had made 45 nuclear detonations to the Soviets' five. The United States was also confident that its bomber fleet was superior in number, speed and range to that of the Soviets. To top it off, the U.S. government was building the distant early warning (DEW) line of radar stations across the Alaskan and Canadian arctic to defend itself against a Soviet surprise bomber attack. However, that confidence and sense of safety quickly began to erode.

There were signs that the Soviets were catching up. To begin with, the Russians detonated their first hydrogen bomb in 1953, only a year after America detonated its first. Still, as with the Soviets' first regular atom bomb in 1949, their success could be attributed more to their adeptness at stealing U.S. secrets than to their own scientific and technological prowess.

But then, during the 1954 May Day military parade in Moscow, foreign observers were startled to see a new, swept-wing, long-range bomber. Called the M-4—and designated Bison by NATO—this new plane could fly long distances at an estimated speed of over 600 mph. Before the M-4, the DEW line provided a four-hour warning of a Soviet surprise attack; the M-4 cut that to two hours. Worse, analysts believed that the Soviets were nearer to full-scale production of this new bomber than the United States was for its new bomber, the B-52.

Analysts predicted that by 1955 the Soviets would have twice as many M-4s as the United States had B-52s. This was confirmed on Red Air Force Day when an American military attache watched wave upon wave of M-4s fly overhead, twice as many as the United States thought existed. It was later discovered that this demonstration was a hoax. The Soviets simply had the same planes circle around and fly overhead over and over again. No one knew that then, however, and thus began the "bomber gap"—the American belief that the Soviets had more bombers than they did.

It became imperative that the United States find out what the Soviets were doing behind their borders. What President Dwight Eisenhower feared most was another surprise attack like the Japanese sudden blitz of Pearl Harbor in December 1941. That attack crippled the American Navy as the United States entered World War II. The question was: Were the Soviets building the capability for such a devastating first strike? No one knew. So, in 1954, Eisenhower assembled what was officially called the Technological Capabilities Panel and was commonly called the Surprise Attack Panel. There were three project teams on the panel: one devoted to offensive needs, another to defensive needs and a third to intelligence needs.

The intelligence subcommittee, called Project Three, was led by Dr. Edwin Land, inventor of the Polaroid Land Camera, and Edward Purcell of Harvard, the Nobel Prize winner for physics in 1952. Project Three reiterated what many in the Air Force and the CIA already knew: It was vital that the United States begin reconnaissance flights directly over the then-denied areas of the Soviet Union. The problem was that there was still no plane that could do the job.

A REVOLUTIONARY AIRPLANE

The Air Force had already decided what it needed in the way of a reconnaissance airplane—a craft that could fly at 70,000 feet over long distances. In March 1953 they issued a design requirement for such a plane to Bell Aircraft and Fairchild (the Air Force didn't include the big companies, like Hughes, Douglas and Boeing, assuming they wouldn't treat what would amount to a small-order plane seriously). Bell and Fairchild began work on their designs and the project was dubbed Bald Eagle.

One company the Air Force didn't bother contacting was Lockheed. An aircraft designer at Lockheed, however, was interested in designing a plane to meet the Air Force requirements. His name was Clarence "Kelly" Johnson and he headed up Lockheed's Advanced Development Projects division. During the war Johnson had been the man behind America's first jet fighter, the F-80, designing and producing the first plane in 141 days. He was also responsible for the C-130 Hercules cargo transport, still the workhorse of the Air Force, and the revolutionary F-104 Starfighter. In 1953 he began to tinker around with the idea of a spy plane.

The main obstacle to building such a plane was the altitude requirement. At 70,000 feet air is so thin that an airplane's engine will only produce 6% of the thrust it does at sea level. This means that the engine has to work very hard at that height. But, the harder it works, the more fuel it consumes, meaning that more fuel will have to be carried. This, however, increases the weight and, in turn, the demands on the engine. There are other problems as well: How will a plane handle in the thin air of 70,000 feet? Will the fuel vaporize because of the low atmospheric pressure and cause the engine to seize up?

Johnson's solution was deceptively simple. He would use an extremely powerful, efficient engine, and he would mount it on a plane with incredible lift characteristics. What he proposed was basically a jet-powered glider. Johnson took his design (he called the plane the CL-282) to the Air Force. They turned him down. They didn't think the engine he proposed using would be up to the task, and anyway, they had their own project, Bald Eagle, with designs coming in from Bell and Fairchild.

Johnson was not about to give up on the CL-282, however. He sidestepped the Air Force brass and took his plan to Trevor Gardiner, the technical adviser to the Air Force's Research and Development division. Gardiner was impressed. Knowing that the way was blocked in the Air Force, he took the design directly to the Project Three intelligence subcommittee of the Surprise Attack Panel. The leaders of Project Three, Edwin Land and Edward Purcell, liked what they saw. They took Johnson's design directly to the CIA's director, Allen Dulles. Dulles was sold, but he knew that the Air Force had to be included in the project, so he assigned a special assistant, Richard Bissell, to sell it to the Air Force brass.

Bissell had been an economics professor at the Massachusetts Institute of Technology when he was recruited into the CIA in the early 1950s. Setting his brilliant mind up to the task of intelligence, he rose fast within the agency. Bissell was enthralled with the possibilities Johnson's plane offered. Like others in the agency, he had always been distrustful of HUMINT—HUman INTelligence, or information gathered by flesh-and-blood agents. One never knew when one was being tricked by a double agent or misled by skewed information. A high-flying spy plane offered "hard" intelligence. Bissell lobbied hard, finally gaining the support of Secretary of the Air Force Harold Talbott. With that, the Air Force's own reconnaissance plane program, Bald Eagle, ended.

There was one more person who had to be convinced— President Eisenhower. On the day before Thanksgiving 1954, Land, Purcell and Dulles took the spy-plane proposal into the Oval Office. Eisenhower was predisposed to like the idea. He knew how valuable photo reconnaissance had been during World War II and, like Bissell, he too preferred technical means of intelligence gathering to HUMINT. Project Three had already expressed to him the belief that America should use the most advanced technology, perhaps even satellites, to spy on the Soviet Union. This spy plane was a good short-term solution. Eisenhower was nervous, as was everyone involved, with the idea of spying on the Soviet Union from the air, but he gave his approval on the spot.

PUTTING IT TOGETHER

Bissell was summoned to the White House that afternoon. As he later noted, it was fine that Dulles had gained Eisenhower's approval to build the plane but no one knew how much it would cost, where the money would come from, where the plane would be built and tested or even who would fly it. Providing answers to those questions became Bissell's job.

Eisenhower wanted the CIA to run the spy plane program. Although himself a military man, he wanted a civilian agency to handle all intelligence gathering. He didn't want the military controlling the means of gathering intelligence in areas that affected it; for example, the number of Soviet bombers and missiles a U.S. spy plane spotted would, in part, determine how big a budget the Air Force would get. Eisenhower feared a conflict of interest. While the Air Force agreed with this arrangement in the beginning, in later years, the issue of who would operate the spy planes—the Air Force or the CIA—would become a bitter debate.

Bissell's first stop was the Pentagon, where he informed Trevor Gardiner of the go-ahead. Not wanting to incur the Air Force's wrath, Bissell first outlined it as a joint project, with the funding coming from Dulles' discretionary account at the agency and some of the materials, including the engines, to come from the Air Force.

Gardiner called Kelly Johnson at Lockheed and gave him the news. Johnson was eager to start. He cleared out a hangar in Burbank, California, and moved in a crew of 23 engineers. They started work almost immediately.

The overall project name was Aquatone. The plane's code name was Idealist. On the drafting paper it was simply called the Utility-2, or U-2. The engineers just called it the Angel. Their work area at Lockheed had been dubbed "Skunk Works" (the name of the clandestine distillery in the Li'l Abner comic strip by Al Capp) in 1953 when the fumes of a nearby plastics factory wafted over. A top-secret outfit in 1954, Lockheed now proudly touts the Skunk Works facility in its promotional material.

As Johnson and the Skunk Works crew began working, Bissell had another task to attend to. Having a plane that could fly over the Soviet Union at 70,000 feet wasn't enough. Also needed were cameras and film that could take pictures from such a height.

Bissell went to Edwin Land of Polaroid, one of the members of the Surprise Attack Panel, a man with full knowledge of the state-of-the-art of photography. He knew who should build the camera, the Hycon Corporation of California. Working from a design by Land and Dr. James Baker, the Harvard astronomer and optics expert that George Goddard had worked with in the 1930s, Hycon came up with a huge piece of equipment, the "B-camera," which was built specifically to fit into the fuselage of the U-2.

The lens that Baker designed was the most revolutionary feature of the camera. Lenses are, in part, rated by their resolving power, the number of black lines per millimeter against a white background the lens can make clear. An average human eye, unaided, can see about 10 lines per millimeter. During the war, Baker produced a lens that could resolve 12 to 15 lines per millimeter. For the U-2, he devised a lens that could discern 50 to 60 lines per millimeter.

A new type of film was designed for the plane as well. Mylar-based, it was thin as plastic wrap, which would allow thousands and thousands of feet of film to be taken up on each flight. The film was also extraordinarily refined and designed to show 100 lines per millimeter. With such film, Baker's lens and the long focal length of the huge Hycon B-camera, the U-2 would be able to pick out something the size of a pack of cigarettes from eight miles in the air. From the operational height of 13 miles it would be able to spot a newspaper page.

From 13 miles, the U-2 would be able to photograph a swath of ground 750 miles wide for general reconnaissance. When the photos required higher resolution, the camera would be able to cover a strip 150 miles across. Because of the extreme thinness of the Mylar film, enough film could be taken aboard to photograph the entire United States in 12 flights.

With the plane in development and the reconnaissance package being assembled, Bissell's next question to answer was what would be done with the pictures after they were taken?

Ray Cline, a former deputy director of the CIA, in his book, *Secrets, Spies and Scholars*, called Richard Bissell "one of the authentic heroes of the intelligence profession" for his work in running the U-2 program. He used almost the exact words to describe Arthur C. Lundahl, the man who oversaw the photo interpretation of the pictures taken from the U-2.

Lundahl was a major booster of photo reconnaissance. He'd been a photo interpreter during the war and had seen the type of intelligence photo reconnaissance could deliver. After the war, he lobbied hard on its behalf. In his book, Ray Cline called Lundahl "the super salesman of photo interpretation." Lundahl became known for rephrasing an old proverb often attributed to the ancient Chinese. Lundahl would say that a picture is worth more than a thousand words: it's worth a thousand spies.

There being little work in the field of photo interpretation after the war, Lundahl turned to teaching. In 1953 he was working at the University of Chicago, teaching photo interpretation and photogrammetry (the science of determining the dimensions of objects in photographs) when the CIA approached him to run a small PI unit for them. Lundahl jumped at the chance. In December 1954 he expanded his small unit when the CIA asked him to oversee interpreting the huge amount of film that the U-2 would bring in. Lundahl moved his operations to a nondescript space above an auto repair shop in a rundown section of Washington, D.C. This was the forerunner to the National Photo Interpretation Center (NPIC) that analyzes the overhead spy photos of today.

Bissell had everything under control. The camera package was being assembled, and Lundahl was putting together a photo interpretation operation. All they needed now was the airplane.

One of the alluring aspects of Kelly Johnson's proposal was that he said he could have the first plane ready to fly in eight months. This seemed a stupendous task, but, with Johnson's track record, it was believed that he just might be able to do it. He did. The first U-2 was ready for testing in July 1955, right on schedule.

The U-2 spy plane on a runway, getting ready for takeoff. Note the pogos supporting the wings. [U.S. Air Force]

THE ANGEL FLIES

The plane was shipped in crates to Groom Lake, Nevada, a dry lake bed near the Yucca Flat nuclear test site. When it was put together the U-2 must have looked strange to the people who saw it for the first time. With an 80-foot wingspan it must have seemed to be all wing. And it must have looked fragile. A rumor circulated that the U-2 was so delicate that each plane could only be used once. Its fragile appearance belied its astonishing capabilities.

The first U-2 flight on July 29, 1955, was an accident. Test pilot Tony LeVier was only supposed to take it along the

A U-2 pilot breathing oxygen and being checked before a flight. [U.S. Air Force]

runway to see how it rolled, but the long wings created so much lift that the thing took to the air.

Flying the U-2 was no easy matter. To simplify the plane the cockpit wasn't pressurized; therefore pilots had to wear full pressure suits, not unlike what astronauts a few years later would wear. They would also have to breathe oxygen. The oxygen prevented the "bends," the same condition that scuba divers encounter if they rise too fast through the water. Tiny bubbles of nitrogen in the blood, if not allowed to dissipate naturally in a slow ascent, will expand and collect in the joints, causing crippling pain. So, before each flight a pilot would spend an hour or more breathing oxygen to flush all the nitrogen out of his blood.

The suit itself was a major annoyance. It took a half-hour just to get into it, and it was terribly uncomfortable. Some pilots found themselves bleeding from chafing at the joints caused by the suit. The suits were designed in a way that didn't allow the pilots to drink, so by the end of a 12-hour flight, the pilots would be dehydrated.

Once all the pilot preparations had been completed following the high-protein, low-residue breakfast (there was no bathroom on board), the oxygen breathing and the suiting up, and once the plane had been checked out, the pilot would be driven out to the airplane and helped into the cockpit. He might have to wait there a while, baking in his suit, longing for the cool, high altitudes, as the final checks were made. When all was ready, the true adventure of flying a U-2 began.

Taking off was not easy. The U-2 had what is known as "bicycle" landing gear: two wheels in line under the fuselage, similar to what gliders have. This meant that the plane had no stability while on the ground. To keep it from tipping over onto one wing, the U-2 had what were called "pogos," sticks with wheels on the end that were used to prop up the ends of the wings. During takeoff, two crewmen, one for each pogo, would sit on the ends of the wings as the plane began to roll. When it built up a little speed, a few miles an hour, enough to stabilize the plane, the crewmen released the pogos, jumped off the wings and moved clear. As the pilot opened up on the throttle, the combination of the immensely powerful engine and the incredible lift of the wings would fling the plane into the air. This part of takeoff has been likened by U-2 pilots to a catapult launch off an aircraft carrier.

This takeoff routine posed dangers. One fatal accident occurred when a pilot discovered that one of his pogos hadn't disengaged. In an attempt to loosen it he flew back over the airfield, wiggling the plane's wings to shake it free. In the process he lost control of the plane and crashed.

Airborne, one of the first disconcerting things that a U-2 pilot would discover was that the long, slender wings flapped up and down. He would also learn that the engine was prone to flameouts at high altitudes. Although having an engine—the plane's one and only engine—conk out at 70,000 feet must have been unnerving, all the pilot had to do was glide to a lower altitude, where the air was thicker, and restart. Other jet planes of the day would've dropped like rocks if their engines failed, but the U-2 was built to glide for miles and miles. Indeed, on spy missions, pilots would sometimes use this gliding ability to conserve on fuel—they'd shut down the engines and just coast for a while.

Despite its gawky appearance, the U-2 actually handled well and could turn quite sharply if needed. After climbing to altitude on a spy mission, the plane would usually be put on autopilot. This allowed it to fly straighter and steadier than human hands could manage—something the cameras required—and enabled the pilot to activate cameras and other spy equipment and to make observations.

Even though the plane would be on autopilot, the pilot still had concerns. One was stability. With the fuel tanks stored in the wings, he had to make sure that the tanks were used equally so that the plane wouldn't list to one side. He was also concerned with maintaining a steady velocity. In the thin air of the high altitudes there was often a very narrow margin between stall and buffet. Stall occurs when the plane's forward velocity drops below a certain speed and the plane suddenly loses lift. Buffet occurs when the plane goes too fast and loses aerodynamic control, no longer cutting through the air but smashing against it. The margin between buffet and stall could be so narrow at 70,000 feet that, on a turn, the outer wing, moving slightly faster, would go into buffet while the inner wing, moving slightly slower, would begin to stall.

Taking off and flying a U-2 proved difficult. Landing it was even harder. First, there was the simple matter of getting it down on the runway. It simply wouldn't go down. The plane's long wings generated so much ground effect, a buildup of air pressure between the wing and the ground, that the pilots would get the U-2 down to the last several feet and find it would go no further. They had to throttle all the way down, and in effect, intentionally try to stall the plane to get it to drop the last few feet.

At the same time, they had to try to keep the plane as steady and level as possible, for it was landing on the two-wheel bicycle gear. The wings had thick metal skids on their tips to prevent the wings from being damaged when the planes tipped to one side. The pilots would wager with one another to see who could keep their plane from tipping over onto one wing for as long as possible. The goal was to keep the plane so steady that the crewmen could run in and slip the pogos under the wing tips before the plane tipped to one side.

Even with the flapping wings, flameouts, stall/buffet problems and difficulties in landing, the pilots generally liked to fly the U-2. In his book *Operation Overflight*, Gary Powers, the one U-2 pilot who would have the misfortune of becoming front-page news, wrote: "There was only one thing wrong with flying higher than any other man had ever flown—you couldn't brag about it."

Powers and the other pilots were officially civilian employees of Lockheed. This was in keeping with Eisenhower's desire that the program be civilian rather than military. The rule was so strict that military pilots recruited to fly the U-2s had to resign their commissions in order to join the program. This was an elite group of flyers. There were only eight in the first group to be trained. They were attracted by the chance to fly an exotic, top-secret plane that had never been flown before. There was undoubtedly a patriotic appeal as well as a financial appeal. Pilots earned $30,000 a year, roughly what an airline captain was making then, and well over $100,000 a year in today's dollars.

Satisfied with the way the plane tested out, Bissell ordered another 22 planes, at a cost of $350,000 each. As Johnson's crew built the planes throughout the latter half of 1955, the pilots trained in Nevada. By early 1956 the planes were rolling out of Skunk Works and the pilots were ready. The time had come to put the spy plane to work.

THE OVERFLIGHTS

Eisenhower would have preferred not to have had to spy on the Soviet Union from the air. At the Geneva Summit Conference in July 1955, just as the U-2 began its testing, Eisenhower made what is known as the "Open Skies" proposal for the prevention of nuclear war. He suggested that the United States and the Soviet Union exchange blueprints of their military facilities and that each country should be allowed to fly over the other to inspect the installations. Some felt this was a bold peace initiative. Others saw it as an American military ploy to get better targeting information. Khrushchev leaned toward the latter interpretation, dismissing Open Skies as a blatant plan for spying.

This didn't entirely matter to the United States, for soon it would possess the unilateral ability to fly over the Soviet Union, with impunity.

As the U-2 program progressed there were several public sightings of this strange plane, and so, a cover story had to be concocted. In 1956, a press release from the National Advisory Committee for Aeronautics (NACA) stated that it had contracted with Lockheed to build the plane for "upper atmosphere research." In keeping with this cover story, in early 1956, three "weather reconnaissance squadrons" were dispatched to Air Force bases in West Germany, Japan and Turkey.

The Incirlik Air Force Base, just outside of Adana, Turkey, was primarily used as a refueling stop for U.S. military planes. The busy activity of the base provided good cover for the 10-10 Detachment—the "weather reconnaissance squadron"—housed in a hangar far away from the others.

The first U-2 missions showed caution and hesitancy. They just skirted the border of the Soviet Union, allowing the cameras to photograph any border installations while the ELINT-gathering devices picked up radio and radar signals. These missions, of course, could just as easily have been performed by RB-47s or Sabrejet reconnaissance planes. The U-2 had been designed for a somewhat more special mission.

In early June 1956 Allen Dulles and Bissell went to Eisenhower with the news that they were ready to begin exploiting the full capabilities of the U-2; they were ready to start the overflights. Eisenhower, always cautious, took time to make his decision. He sent word the next day: They had a 10-day period in which to spy on Russia.

For the first four days the Soviet Union was socked in with cloud cover. On the fifth day the clouds cleared and a U-2 took off on the first overflight. Dulles called Bissell to see if the plane had indeed gotten off the ground. Bissell replied that it had, and that it was in the air as they spoke. Dulles asked about the flight plan and was told that the plane would fly over Moscow and Leningrad. Dulles was taken aback: Was that wise, on the first flight? Bissell replied that it would be easier on that flight than on any other.

Unfortunately for the United States, one major intelligence find of the first flight was that Soviet radar was better than they thought. It had been believed that the U-2 might be undetectable by the Soviets, that it would fly too high for their radar to reach. They were wrong. The plane triggered radar alerts right across the country. MiGs and SAMs—surface-to-air missiles—tried to bring the Angel down, but fell short. The Soviets were furious. They confined their screaming and yelling to diplomatic channels, in part because they didn't want to admit publicly that they were powerless to stop the plane. Eisenhower, chastened by their response, suspended the flights planned for the following month. From then on he would approve them one at a time.

There were two types of overflight: those that followed a looping pattern and others that were straight shots, going right across the country from one side to another. These straight-shot flights were different from any reconnaissance flights the pilots had ever flown. As an early U-2 pilot noted, these missions weren't like some reconnaissance missions that were flown in World War II or Korea where the pilot decided that it was too dangerous to take pictures over the target, so he made the excuse the weather was too bad and returned home. Once you got started over the Soviet Union in a U-2 you had no place to go but your destination.

Of course, the U-2 was designed so that these flights would specifically avoid danger. The planes were built to fly at 70,000 feet because Soviet SAMs were thought incapable of reaching over 60,000 feet. The conservative estimate was that the U-2 would have a two-year lifespan before the Soviets built a rocket that could reach it. Ultimately, the U-2 was able to fly over the Soviet Union for four years, twice as long as had been planned, and, as it happened, a little longer than was safe.

A U-2 in flight. [U.S. Air Force]

3

THE U-2 IN CRISIS

They didn't talk much about the idea of a plane being shot down, but provisions had been made just in case it did happen. A pack in the ejection seat contained a number of items that would help a pilot survive—a collapsible life raft, clothing, food, water, compass, flares, matches, chemicals for starting a fire with damp wood, and a first-aid kit with morphine, bandages, dressings and water purification tablets. There was also a silk American flag bearing a message in 14 languages: "I am an American and do not speak your language. I need food, shelter, assistance. I will not harm you. I bear no malice toward your people. If you help me you will be rewarded." For reward money there were 7,500 rubles, 24 gold Napoleon francs and a small selection of wristwatches and rings, worth, all told, something over $1,000. In addition, the pack contained a knife and a .22 caliber pistol with a silencer.

There was one other, rather peculiar item in the ejection-seat pack, a curious silver dollar good luck charm. Was it another trinket a pilot was to use to barter for freedom? No. An inch-long pin concealed in the coin was coated with curare, a poison that kills by relaxing all muscles, including the heart and lungs. This wasn't a diabolical weapon but a means of escape. In light of the harrowing tales that came out of the Korean War, tales of torture and brainwashing, the pilots were given the pin in order to kill themselves.

This pin figured prominently in subsequent events for it begged the question: Were the pilots expected to kill themselves to avoid interrogation? By all accounts they were never told to commit suicide upon capture. In fact, one CIA official thought that a pilot might as well tell his captors everything he knew. For one thing, the pilots didn't know that much. The day before a flight a pilot would be shown a color-coded map that showed his primary route in blue, with red dots showing where he was to turn on the various reconnaissance equipment. Brown lines indicated the way to other American bases if he had to break off the flight for any reason. The pilots were never told the purpose of their mission, nor did they, except on rare occasions, see the pictures they had taken.

While the pilots were never told that they had to kill themselves, they were told to destroy the plane. To that end, U-2s were fitted with a two-and-a-half-pound explosive destruct unit, not big enough to destroy the whole plane, but hopefully large enough to wipe out the incriminating reconnaissance equipment. A pilot in a plane going down was supposed to activate the destruct unit, which was on a 70-second delay, then eject himself clear of the aircraft.

Things don't always turn out as planned.

THE U-2 INCIDENT

"One of NASA's U-2 research planes, in use since 1956 in a continuing program to study gust-meterological conditions found at high altitude, has been missing since about 9 o'clock Sunday morning (local time) when its pilot reported he was having oxygen difficulties over the Lake Van, Turkey area...If the pilot continued to suffer lack of oxygen, the path of the airplane from the last reported position would be impossible to determine. If the airplane was on automatic pilot, it is likely it would have continued along its northeasterly course."

That is an excerpt from the press release issued after a U-2 disappeared on May 1, 1960. The press release had a few things wrong, of course. The plane wasn't flying over Turkey, it was flying over the Soviet Union. And it wasn't studying "gust-meteorological conditions," it was spying.

By the spring of 1960, President Eisenhower was being very stingy about okaying requests for more flights. He knew that there was a huge backlog of photos from previous missions that hadn't even been looked at yet. And he didn't want to rile the Soviets unnecessarily with additional flights until that backlog had been examined. The flights were also dangerous. No one knew how long it would be before the inevitable happened and a U-2 would be shot down.

By 1958 the U-2 flight planners were already routing the plane away from known sites of the new generation of Soviet SAMs, the SA-2 Guidelines. These new SAMs were not expected to reach much above 60,000 feet, but it was feared that a lucky shot, combined with a U-2 dipping below its optimum altitude, could spell disaster. The intelligence community tried to get as many flights in as it could before the Soviets finally did knock one down.

Bissell went to Eisenhower with another flight request in April 1960. Also present was Secretary of State Christian Herter, who did not like the idea. A summit meeting of the superpowers was scheduled for Paris in the early part of May and Herter didn't want to jeopardize it. He did not think it would be a good time for a U-2 to be shot down over the Soviet Union. Eisenhower felt that no time would be a good time for a U-2 to be shot down over the Soviet Union and gave his approval. Bissell had two weeks.

For two weeks there was no break in the cloud cover over the Soviet Union. Bissell asked for an extension and Eisenhower gave it, *with* the provision that on no account could the flight take place after May 2—any later would be too close to the summit.

Instead of taking off from Turkey, the plane was scheduled to depart from a second base the 10-10 Detachment used in Peshawar, a city set in the dry highlands of Pakistan. Like Bissell, who was half a world away, the pilot and crew waited for the clouds to part. The pilot selected for this mission was Francis Gary Powers, one of the first pilots to be trained on the U-2 in 1955. The days passed, with no letup in the weather, as the May 2 deadline approached. Finally, on the last day of April, word came that the clouds over the spy targets were expected to clear the next day. Bissell gave the green light and the crew in Peshawar mobilized into action.

Ironically, the plane flew on May 1, one of the most important days on the Soviet calendar. For communist people around the world, May Day celebrates the "worker" and "class struggle." It is a day of parades, the biggest of which is the Soviet Red Army's parade of military might through Red Square in Moscow. For Americans, an equivalent celebration would be a combination of the Fourth of July and Veteran's Day. It was strangely appropriate that this would be the day that the Angel would make its last overflight of the Soviet Union.

At 5:20 A.M., May 1, Gary Powers, already hot and uncomfortable in his pressure suit, climbed into the cockpit of a U-2 on the runway at Peshawar. He'd been up for hours, eating breakfast, breathing oxygen and donning the suit. Once in the cockpit, there was a delay and Powers baked in his suit for another 20 minutes. At 6:20 A.M. the plane began its roll, gathered speed, dropped the pogos and rocketed off into the early light over the Karakoram foothills.

About an hour after takeoff Powers crossed the Soviet border, triggering radar alerts. The word went out across the Soviet Union that yet another plane had violated Soviet airspace. MiGs took off to dog the U-2, getting as close to it as they could. Antiaircraft units along the U-2's projected course were mobilized. One of these was situated near Sverdlovsk, a major city and military center about 800 miles east of Moscow.

Powers was pleased as he neared Sverdlovsk. The flight, near its halfway point, so far had been uneventful. In the middle of a 90-degree turn 30 miles out of Sverdlovsk,

Powers spotted an airfield that wasn't on his maps. In addition to turning the cameras and other spy equipment on and off, pilots were also supposed to watch for anything interesting. So, Powers made a note of it. He then checked that all the spy equipment was operating properly, then took a look at his flight instrumentation dials.

Suddenly, without warning, the plane was hit. In his book on the incident, *Operation Overflight*, Powers recounted his impressions. "I can remember feeling, hearing and just sensing an explosion. I immediately looked up from the instrument panel and everywhere I looked it was orange. I said 'My God, I've had it now.'"

The plane started to drop, nose up, very quickly. All Powers could see was spinning blue sky. He couldn't fire the ejection seat from the position he'd ended up in after the explosion. Ejecting would have taken his legs off, so he had to try to bail out manually.

Time was running out. By the time he realized he'd have to bail out, the plane had already dropped 30,000 feet. He knew he had to arm the destruct unit. But he didn't know how long it would take to bail out, and he didn't want to be in the plane when the charge went off. His plan: Release the canopy, pop the seat belt, get set to jump free, then flip the destruct switches. It almost worked.

Powers jettisoned the canopy and it whipped off out of sight. But the second he popped open his belt release he shot out of the cockpit. He wasn't thrown free. His oxygen hose held firm, giving him a last chance to reach back into the plane and arm the destruct unit. Easier said than done. Powers was sprawled over the nose of a U-2 tumbling down wildly over the Soviet Union. Blinded by a faceplate that had frozen over the instant he shot out of the plane, he tried to reach back in for the destruct switches, which were just beyond his stretching fingers. Every second that passed brought him 300 feet closer to the ground. Now he only had time to save himself.

He lunged against the oxygen hose. It didn't break. He strained, again and again, until, finally, it snapped.

Powers broke free. The rushing air pulled him up and away from the plummeting plane. He dropped several thousand feet before he remembered his ripcord. Just as he reached for it, the automatic barometric control released the parachute. The canopy opened, billowing up above him. As he drifted down he watched the U-2 crash some distance away. He had a decision to make. Powers took out the silver dollar with the curare-coated pin concealed inside. What should he do—should he kill himself? Powers still harbored some hope that he might be able to escape, so he threw the pin away.

Within moments of landing on Soviet soil, Powers was surrounded by a group of farmers who helped him gather up his parachute. They spoke a language he did not understand and eyed him with curious bemusement. Minutes later he was met by more official representatives who had been notified by the local antiaircraft unit that they had brought down a prized plane. Within hours Powers was in Moscow, in a KGB jail cell in the Lubyanka prison.

The Soviets knew they had a powerful hand and they played their cards judiciously. They didn't tell the world they had Powers, they just said they'd shot down a spy plane. The United States, of course, denied everything, steadfastly maintaining that the plane had been an atmospheric research craft. The Americans accused the Soviets of shooting down an innocent plane in cold blood. It was then that Soviet Premier Nikita Khrushchev played his trump card: The pilot was alive.

With Powers, the recovered plane wreckage, the mangled, but still identifiable reconnaissance equipment and the spy esoterica (most notably the silver coin with the curare-coated pin, which was recovered from the field), the Soviets had incontrovertible proof that the Americans had been spying on them. Not only had they finally brought down a U-2, effectively ending the program, they had also caught the

United States in a lie, a major victory for the Soviets in the ongoing international propaganda war between the two superpowers.

The incident had the feared effect on the Paris summit conference. In *Secret Sentries in Space,* author Philip Klass quoted the main participants of the conference from the official record. In his opening remarks, Khrushchev harangued the United States for the incident, ending with the exclamation, "I have been overflown!" In an effort to dampen the emotion and bring some reason to the matter, French president Charles de Gaulle, the host of the summit, quietly remarked that he, too, had been overflown—by a Soviet satellite. Khrushchev protested that it had been an innocent satellite. De Gaulle asked him how it brought back photographs of the far side of the Moon. Khrushchev replied, begrudgingly, "In that satellite we had cameras." De Gaulle nodded. "Ah, in that one you had cameras! Pray, continue."

But Khrushchev did not continue and he and his entourage soon stormed out of the meeting.

As the fallout from the incident continued to rain down, Eisenhower promised that the United States would never again overfly the Soviet Union. Except for the occasional border-crossing sortie, the United States has, for the most part, lived up to the pledge. Officially no planes have crossed the Soviet Union (that, of course, does not include satellites).

In Washington, as the Eisenhower administration and the intelligence community tried to pick up the pieces after the incident, the strongest reaction to the downing of the plane was anger, and a lot of the anger was directed at Powers. People wondered if he'd been flying too low, and they were upset that he hadn't set off the destruct unit. Some were even angry that he hadn't killed himself.

Powers always maintained that he wasn't flying too low, but that he'd been the victim of a near miss, which was certainly within the capability of that new generation of Soviet SAMs. It is believed that the Soviets were so frustrated at their inability to bring a U-2 down that they sent up barrages of SAMs, hoping that one might be able to break through. There was even a report that they sent up so many missiles that one of them took out a MiG that was dogging the U-2, killing the pilot.

As for the criticism that Powers didn't arm the destruct unit, some have argued that it didn't matter; there was no guarantee that even a two-pound explosive charge could destroy all the cameras and the large, tightly wound roll of spy film. As for Powers not killing himself, what would have been the point? Pilots could reveal little except admit that they were indeed spy pilots. But there was so much other evidence to confirm the spy mission (all the contents of the seat pack, such as the gun and silencer) that it didn't matter if the pilot was dead or alive. And, as for propaganda, a dead spy pilot who had poisoned himself with curare would be even more of a black mark against the United States. Still, there were those who remained angry. According to Stephen Ambrose's book on the CIA in the Eisenhower years, *Ike's Spies*, Eisenhower's son John is reported to have exclaimed, "The CIA promised us that the Russians would never get a U-2 pilot alive. And then they gave the S.O.B. a parachute!"

Did the CIA make such a promise? Powers believed that Eisenhower had been told that the pilots had been instructed to kill themselves, even though they had never been given such instruction. The government has denied that Eisenhower was ever told this.

Some suspect that the CIA could promise that no pilot would be caught alive because they had rigged the destruct units without the supposed 70-second delay. They would go off the instant the pilot flipped the switches. Some say that Powers suspected this and that this was the reason he didn't arm the device. Powers, however, always maintained that he was certain there was a delay and that the only reason he didn't arm the device was because he couldn't reach it.

If the CIA did promise that no U-2 pilot would be taken alive it was likely because neither Bissell, nor anyone else involved in the project, imagined that a U-2 would stand one chance in a million of surviving a SAM strike at 70,000 feet.

In the months following the crash, the Soviets mined this vein of propaganda gold for all it was worth. The wreckage of the U-2 was displayed in public and Powers was tried on Soviet national television. Convicted of espionage, he could have received the death penalty, but instead was sentenced to 10 years imprisonment. He was released not long after, however, as part of a spy trade in which the United States got Powers in exchange for Soviet agent Colonel Rudolph Abel, who had been running a spy ring in New York and had been captured in 1957.

After an initial flurry of press attention upon his return, Powers settled down to a private life of relative obscurity. In 1977 there was a sad, tragic final note to the story of the last overflight: Powers died when the helicopter he flew for a Los Angeles-area TV station crashed.

While the U-2 never did fly over the Soviet Union again, it continued to fly over other countries the United States wanted to probe. In one incident, the U-2 played a major role in averting nuclear war.

THE CUBAN MISSILE CRISIS

In the summer of 1962, U.S. spies around the world began to notice that the Soviet Union was shipping an inordinate amount of military hardware to Cuba. The Soviets had been pumping arms into that Caribbean island-nation ever since the corrupt dictatorship of Fulgencio Batista had been over-thrown by Fidel Castro and his revolutionary army in 1959. In the summer of 1962, however, the ship-watchers, employed by the United States, who monitored the choke points of the world—narrow straits, such as the Bosporus in Turkey and the Panama Canal—saw the amount of Soviet military cargo bound for Cuba increase rapidly.

At the National Photographic Interpretation Center (NPIC) in Washington, D.C., Art Lundahl's PIs had a pretty good idea of what was on board the Soviet ships. They had developed a technique they called "cratology": By figuring out the outer dimensions of a crate in a picture taken by a ship-watcher, they could make a good guess of what was inside. That summer, cratology told them the Soviets were sending airplanes and antiaircraft missiles, among other things, to Cuba.

Other signs indicated that something was up in Cuba. Spies working the docks in Cuba spoke of strange cargoes. Many of these accounts were discounted, however, as few persons in the CIA trusted the human-gathered intelligence that came out of Cuba since much of it was exaggerated, wrong or had been planted by Cuban double agents. There was enough suspicion, however, that it was decided that some hard intelligence should be gathered. A U-2 was sent up over the island on August 29. It returned with pictures of eight SAM antiaircraft sites under construction. The question was, why so many, and what were they being built to protect?

A U-2 photograph of a Soviet-constructed surface-to-air missile (SAM) site in Cuba, taken August 29, 1962. [U.S. Air Force]

President John F. Kennedy was worried. There was no way he could allow the Soviets to place nuclear missiles on Cuba, an island only 90 miles from Florida. Kennedy let Soviet Premier Khrushchev know of his concern through diplomatic channels. After some early confrontations, Kennedy and Khrushchev were at that time establishing more cordial relations. Khrushchev assured Kennedy that he wouldn't cause any trouble in a congressional election year and that they would put no missiles in Cuba.

The new CIA director, John McCone, didn't believe Khrushchev. Although he didn't think the Soviets would put missiles in Cuba to use in war, he thought they might put them in to use later as valuable bargaining chips. McCone was alone on this. Others argued that the Soviets had never previously put missiles in a satellite country. McCone answered that the reason they hadn't was that they trusted no one. They wouldn't put IRBMs (intermediate-range ballistic missiles) in Poland or Hungary because the missiles could reach back to Russia, but such missiles in Cuba could only reach the United States. Nevertheless, McCone was outvoted. After repeated U-2 flights revealed no new developments on the island, the U.S. Intelligence Board declared that it was highly unlikely that the Soviets would put missiles on Cuban soil any time soon. McCone asked that his dissenting vote be recorded.

It wasn't long before new reports came in from Cuba. Agents spotted large, open-hatched ships, the kind usually used to carry lumber. However, they were riding higher than usual: Perhaps they were carrying something else? On September 21 an agent even reported seeing a long-range missile on a trailer. The corroborating evidence came when the Defense Intelligence Agency's Colonel John Wright looked at some of the U-2 photos of Cuba. Wright, an expert on Soviet military installations, noticed that the SAM sites on Cuba were set up in the exact same configuration the Soviets used to guard their medium-range ballistic missiles (MRBMs) in the U.S.S.R. This was confirmed by a manual smuggled out of the Soviet Union by Oleg Penkovsky, a high-ranking officer in Soviet military intelligence who was working for the West. The manual detailed how SAM batteries around MRBM sites were to be built—just as they were in Cuba.

On October 4 it was decided that U-2s should again scour the island. Air Force pilots, rather than CIA civilian pilots, would fly the plane due to the threat of war. If a military pilot were to be shot down, he would be treated as a prisoner of war, and not shot as a spy. The CIA lobbied hard to maintain control of the flights, but lost. This was the beginning of the end for the CIA in its quest to control all overhead reconnaissance.

A photograph of a medium-range ballistic missile site near San Cristobal, Cuba, taken by U-2 pilot Captain Richard Heyser on October 14, 1962. [U.S. Air Force]

Cloud cover over Cuba prevented the U-2 from flying for several days. The first one got off the ground on October 14, piloted by Captain Richard Heyser. He managed to take 928 photos and was spared a SAM attack. The moment Heyser landed, the photos were rushed to Art Lundahl and his men at NPIC in Washington. In an article in the October 1977 issue of *American Heritage* on the U-2 and the missile crisis, writer Don Moser quoted many of the principals involved in the crisis. According to Moser's article, on October 15, one of the PIs called Lundahl at home and asked him to come in. "We want you to look at something," he said.

When Lundahl walked in, no one said a word to him (PIs don't want to influence what another PI might see in a photo). Lundahl got his stereoscopic glasses and went over to the light table. He adjusted his glasses and there, jumping off the photo in 3D were palm trees, jungle ground slashed by the tracks of heavy equipment, empty missile transporters, blast deflectors, cherry-picker cranes, long rectangular missile tents and Soviet nuclear weapon transportation vans.

Photo-interpreters going over the U-2 photos taken of Cuba during the missile crisis. [U.S. Air Force]

In Moser's article, Lundahl recalled that he looked at the PIs in the room. "Okay, I know what you're thinking, and you're right. This is a medium-range ballistic missile site. I don't want you to leave this room. Call your wives, break up your car pools. Do it casually. But stay in this room."

Lundahl couldn't reach McCone, but he did get Deputy Director of the CIA Ray Cline. He told Cline they'd found evidence of two MRBM sites in Cuba with missiles ready for deployment—missiles that, with their 1,020-mile range, could reach Washington, D.C.

Cline, in turn, called presidential assistant McGeorge Bundy at home. There was no scrambler on the line, so Cline spoke in broad, cryptic terms. "You know that island we were talking about the other day? Well, they've got some big ones."

Bundy caught on. "Are they ready to shoot?"

"No, but they are rapidly approaching it."

Bundy called Kennedy. The president was furious that Khrushchev had lied to him. When Cline and Lundahl arrived at the White House with the incriminating photographs, Kennedy looked at the photos with a magnifying glass but couldn't identify what he was seeing. No one in that room October 16 who looked at the photos could see what Lundahl saw. To the untrained eye it was just trees with some dots and lines thrown in. Kennedy asked Lundahl if he was sure.

In Moser's article, Lundahl recalled what he said to the president. "It could be a papier-mache world out there, but I'm as sure of this as a photo interpreter can be."

With that, the Cuban Missile Crisis, as it came to be known, began. If the Soviets didn't pull the missiles out, Kennedy knew that he would have to order an invasion of Cuba. But the Soviets might then launch the weapons in retaliation and to prevent their capture, and that could well have signaled the start of World War III. Instead of invasion, Kennedy opted for the intermediate step of a naval blockade of Cuba, which would prevent more equipment from reaching the island while at the same time allow time for negotiations.

During those two tense weeks in October, U-2s continued to scour the island, checking for any changes. There were also a number of low-altitude reconnaissance missions with pilots flying RF-101 Voodoos. These were called "jinking" missions. The unarmed planes would scream in low at 500 mph, doing rolls and hard, stomach-churning turns to evade the antiaircraft flak, straighten out in order to take the pictures, then scream off again. On October 27, a U-2 was shot down over Cuba and the pilot was killed. Was it an accident or were the Soviets preparing to launch?

A low-level reconnaissance photo take from a RF-101 Voodoo of a San Cristobal MRBM site. [U.S. Air Force]

The crisis heightened. The next day, Khrushchev announced that they would dismantle the launch sites and take back the weapons. As part of the secret deal, the United States would dismantle obsolete nuclear missile sites in Turkey, which would allow Khrushchev to save some face at home.

In the following weeks U-2s monitored the Soviet withdrawal to make sure that they really were removing the missiles. They were. The crisis passed, and the photographs taken from the U-2 and analyzed at NPIC had been instrumental in resolving it.

4

THE SR-71 BLACKBIRD

The U-2 was originally designed as an interim method for spying on the Soviet Union, something that eventually would be replaced by spy satellites. But based on the U-2's success, it became apparent that spy planes could play an invaluable role in intelligence gathering. However, the U-2 was also limited; any country with SAMs could bring one down. So, if the United States was to have a useful spy plane, it would have to improve on the U-2's design. For this reason, while the U-2's immediate successor was the spy satellite, its kindred spirit successor was the SR-71—the Blackbird.

The Soviet Union and Cuba weren't the only countries to shoot down U-2s. In the early 1960s, several U-2s flown by Nationalist Chinese (Taiwanese) pilots were shot down over China. Therefore, there was a need for a plane that could fly higher than the SAMs could reach. Flying higher also allowed for broader coverage. One might think that the lower the altitude a spy could fly, the better, but that isn't always true. Certainly an RF-101 Voodoo on a tree-top jinking mission can bring back remarkable photographs, but such missions miss the forest for the trees. Pictures taken from high-flying spy planes permit broader patterns and designs to become apparent; objects appear that could well be lost at lower altitudes.

Another requirement for a successor to the U-2 was that it would have to fly very fast. The U-2, cruising along at a relatively slow subsonic speed of 500 mph or so, was rather easy to spot on radar and track. A new spy plane would have to fly three or four times as fast in order to make it difficult to track on radar and to enable it to outrun missiles launched its way. While the U-2 had a top speed of less than Mach 1 (the speed of sound, roughly 750 mph at sea level), a new spy plane would have to fly at Mach 3.

The CIA and the Air Force turned to a man they knew could build them this remarkable plane: Kelly Johnson.

Johnson's first design, called the CL-400, was really not a plane at all; it was a bullet, a rocket-powered bullet. Called Project Suntan, the idea was to use liquid-fuel rocket technology in the plane's design. Like a missile, it would be fueled by liquid hydrogen. However, it was not to be. Although between $100 million and $250 million was spent in the design stage, Johnson couldn't get the idea to work, and it died on the drafting table.

Johnson wasn't the only one working on the idea of a high-altitude plane. The Navy had plans for a rocket-powered plane that would be lifted to a high altitude by a balloon, then boosted to Mach 3 by rocket engines. One problem: To lift a rocket plane to such an altitude, the balloon would have to be one mile in diameter.

The Convair division of the General Dynamics Corporation (a major military contractor) was able to design a plane that would fly at Mach 4. Like the Navy design, however, it had a problem getting off the ground on its own. So the plan was to lift it to high altitudes by a B-58 bomber, then release it when the bomber reached supersonic speeds. The trouble here: The B-58, although a remarkable plane, would not likely have been able to reach supersonic speeds with an airplane strapped to its belly.

Johnson and the Skunk Works crew came up with a total of 12 designs for this new plane, calling them simply A-1, A-2, etc. The one they finally clicked with was the last, A-12.

Designing a plane such as this presented formidable problems, the most daunting of which was: How do you get a plane to fly that high and that fast? The answer lay in using something that doesn't fly high *and* fast, but high *therefore* fast—the then-theoretical ramjet engine. A ram engine is an almost perpetual motion machine. At a certain speed at high altitude, it uses the force of the thin air ramming into the engine intake to provide the thrust out the back of the engine, requiring only a little fuel mixed with the air to augment the power. In fact, ram engines are not only self-perpetuating, but actually self-increasing; the faster a ram engine goes, the faster it wants to go. If the engines on the SR-71 weren't reigned in, the plane would continue to accelerate indefinitely until it tore itself apart.

The problem with ram engines is that they only work at high speeds at high altitudes; to fly at Mach 1 at sea level with this engine would be like trying to fly a normal plane through water. The Convair design avoided the problem of ram engines at low altitude by having the plane lifted and boosted by a B-58. Johnson wanted to build a plane that could take off and reach the high altitudes and lower ram speeds on its own. So he designed an engine that was both a conventional turbofan jet engine and a ramjet engine. The engine has a movable cone in front of its intake opening. By moving the cone back and forth, changing the airflow into the engine, the engine can work at all speeds.

Heat was the next major design problem to conquer. At Mach 3 (over 2,100 mph) friction caused by air rushing over the plane's hull can create temperatures of well over 800 degrees F. Such temperatures would destroy aluminum, which meant that the plane would have to be made out of stainless steel or titanium. It also meant that new heat-resistant hydraulic fluids, greases and electrical wiring would have to be developed, along with a fuel with a wide range of temperature stability—from -90 degrees F (the temperature it would be during mid-air refueling) to 600 degrees F, the temperature it could reach in the airplane before being fed into the engine's burner.

High temperatures posed other problems—how to keep the cockpit cool enough for a human, and how to prevent the rubber tires on the landing gear from melting or exploding from intense heat inside the tires. The heat might also create trouble for the spy cameras, as photographs taken through a window might be distorted by the hot, turbulent airflow across the glass.

Johnson devised solutions for all of these design problems and made repeated presentations to the CIA and the Air Force. On August 29, 1959, Richard Bissell picked the A-12 from the various competing designs. On January 30, 1960, Johnson was given the go-ahead to begin production.

A SR-71, head on. [U.S. Air Force]

THE SR FLIES

Another Johnson—President Lyndon Johnson—announced to the world on February 29, 1964 that America had a plane that could fly 2,000 mph at an altitude of over 70,000 feet. Keeping with the tradition of giving all reconnaissance planes an "R" prefix (at least those that were openly reconnaissance planes, such as the RB-47 or the RF-101, but not the U-2), Lockheed's A-12 would be called the RS-71A (Reconnaissance/Strike-71A). The story is told that in announcing the plane's existence, President Johnson misspoke and called it the SR-71. As SR could stand for Strategic Reconnaissance, it seemed easier to change the plane's designation than to correct the president, and it stuck.

Today the plane has many names. To the press relations people at Lockheed, the plane is the more romantic-sounding Blackbird. To the men who fly the tanker planes that refuel the SR-71 in flight, it is the Sled because it is so flat. To the Lockheed and Air Force crews who service and fly the plane, it is simply the SR. Whatever it is called, 30 years after its original inception, it is still one of the most remarkable planes in the air.

While Johnson solved the plane's design problems on paper, building it turned out to be a daunting task. The decision was made to make the airplane's skin out of heat-resistant titanium. Titanium, however, is incredibly brittle and hard to work with. Building a watch out of titanium would be one thing, but fashioning a whole plane out of it is quite another. The engineers built their own titanium forge on the Skunk Works premises, and in the course of building the first SRs, advanced the field of titanium metallurgy several steps.

They solved the problem of the potentially exploding tires by filling them with helium, which expands less than air as it is heated. Nevertheless, even helium-filled tires can explode, so when the landing gear retracts after takeoff, the wheels are enclosed in bomb shields in the event one does happen to blow.

An amazing mixture called JP-7 is used for fuel. If you walked into an SR-71 hangar, you might be surprised to see pools of the liquid on the floor around the plane. There's no safety hazard; the fuel does not evaporate and it has a very high ignition point, so high, in fact, that you could put out a cigarette in one of the pools. The pools are not the result of carelessness; they form because seams in the fuel tanks are loose in order that the tanks can expand without buckling when the plane heats up at supersonic speeds.

Like the U-2, the SR-71 is different from most planes. It doesn't have flaps like normal planes to help with landing and takeoff. Instead, there is a narrow ledge, a continuous horizontal fin that runs around the outside of the fuselage, and on takeoff it helps the wing generate enough lift to get the plane airborne. On landing, the plane relies on its ability to create a great deal of ground effect between it and the runway to slow the descent and cushion the final drop.

An SR-71 being refueled in flight. [U.S. Air Force]

During an operational flight, the SR is run almost entirely on autopilot so that it is as stable as possible when pictures are being taken. Hand-flying the plane is not laborious. Although the plane may look exotic, the pilot's cockpit isn't. The only special controls are a center-of-gravity indicator and several controls that are specific to the operation of the ram engines.

The plane was designed with several *stealth* characteristics that help it avoid radar. A very thin plane, the SR doesn't present much in the way of a radar profile, and most of its edges are rounded or angled. Therefore, radar beams glance off rather than bounce back to the radar dishes. And the SR's black outer coating absorbs radar beams. There are also many electronic devices on board, such as radar detectors and jammers, that help it avoid radar detection.

If the plane is spotted and tracked it cannot dodge well. The plane is not agile; it can't make deft maneuvers. At top speed, a 180-degree turn will have a radius of several hundred miles. For example, if an SR was heading west full throttle across the United States toward the Pacific, and it started to turn around over San Francisco, the arc of the turn would take it over the ocean and it would be flying over Los Angeles before it was headed east.

Of course, agility is not really necessary with a plane that flies as high and fast as the SR-71. This plane can go from New York to London in less than two hours. Officially, after almost 30 years, the SR still holds the world aircraft record for speed and altitude: 2,193.6 mph at 85,069 feet. In truth the SR-71 can fly at Mach 4 (2,600 mph or so) at a height of over 100,000 feet.

There are a few Soviet planes and a handful of SAMs that can reach that height. But by the time an enemy plane can take off in pursuit or a missile can be launched, the SR is hundreds of miles away. It moves so fast that planes and missiles can't catch it from behind, and if approaching head-on, they don't have time to adjust to intercept it. There have been several accidents in which SR-71s have been lost, but as far as anyone knows, no SR has ever been brought down by enemy fire.

The purpose of the SR, of course, is not to set records, but to spy on other countries. To do this work the plane has a vast array of reconnaissance systems. Like the U-2 and other recon planes, the SR has replaceable nose configurations so that whole packages of different spy equipment can be

An SR-71 in flight. [U.S. Air Force]

exchanged at once. For basic overhead spy photography, the plane carries two cameras with 48-inch focal lengths. The photographs, taken on a 1,500-foot length of strip film, cover a swath of between 800 and 1,600 nautical miles, bringing back images with ground resolution as high as nine inches. Images may be recorded in black and white, color, and infrared, and they may be monoscopic or stereoscopic. The

SR may also carry SLAR—side-looking synthetic aperture radar—that can produce radar images with a resolution of 10 feet, day or night, in all weather.

In the aftermath of the U-2 incident, the United States vowed never again to send a spy plane over the Soviet Union. Neither side will publicly say whether or not America has lived up to that promise. In all likelihood there probably have been a few overflights, yet they would be few and far between. The SR-71 does most of its spying on the Soviet Union from outside the border. For this reason the SR often flies with an OBC—optical bar camera—with a 30-inch focal length that provides 12-inch resolution of objects far beyond the borders.

In the 1960s designers developed a way to get around the prohibition on overflights. It was called the D-21 drone, a small, pilotless craft that was to be carried up by the SR, then launched over the Soviet border at Mach 4. This photographic bullet would zoom in, take some pictures, then zoom out again, parachuting down for recovery. One D-21 was tested on an SR on July 3, 1966. It caused the plane to crash and the program, as far as the SR was concerned, was terminated. These drones were, however, subsequently launched from B-52s and used to spy on China.

The SR-71 may not be the hardest plane to fly, but it certainly is one of the most prestigious. Of the many who apply for duty aboard an SR-71, few are accepted. Pilots must be young, fit and have at least 1,500 hours of jet-flying time. The RSOs— reconnaissance systems operators—who sit in the second cockpit behind the pilot, must also be in top physical condition and must have at least 2,500 hours of navigation experience on B-52s and B-58s.

In the struggle between the CIA and the Air Force over control of spy plane operations, the CIA finally lost. The SR-71s are flown by the Air Force's Strategic Air Command (SAC). Due to accidents, only 15 to 19 of the planes remain, out of an estimated 30 to 35 that were originally built, each costing $19.6 million. In the 1960s Lockheed had the tooling for the planes destroyed. According to some, it was at the behest of then Secretary of Defense Robert McNamara, who didn't want the SR to compete with a plane system he was backing. Like the condor, the Blackbird faces extinction—when the last one goes, there will be no more.

Even the ones still in use may not be in use much longer. In May 1988, Secretary of the Air Force Edward C. Aldridge, Jr. announced that the Air Force would begin to retire the SRs. Two reasons were given: The SRs are very expensive to fly, with each operation costing hundreds of thousands of dollars; and there is a duplication of effort with the spy satellites.

An RF-4C Phantom II reconnaissance plane, used for low-level tactical reconnaissance, in flight. [U.S. Air Force]

If the SR is retired, there are other spy planes. The U-2 (now called the TR-1) is still in service and it can do the same job as the SR-71 over any country that doesn't possess advanced SAMs. There are also squadrons of ELINT—electronic intelligence—planes, most notably the RC-135s. These planes cruise along the Soviet and Chinese borders, listening for radar and radio transmissions. (An RC-135 was in the vicinity of Korean Airlines Flight 007 when the airliner was shot down by the Soviets in September 1983, and according to one theory, it didn't warn the civilian plane it had gone off course and had entered Soviet airspace because it wanted to see what the Soviet response would be.)

A reconnaissance crew readying cameras in an RF-4C Phantom II. [U.S. Air Force]

There are other spycraft in use, many of which harken back to the original intent of spying from the air, when one general wanted to find out what the enemy was up to on the other side of the hill. For this type of battlefield reconnaissance, the trend points toward remotely piloted vehicles—RPVs—which are small, unmanned camera-packed drones that are sent out over enemy territory to take pictures (some broadcast pictures back; others return with film). There are even small, helicopter-like devices that are used like the spy balloons of the Civil War. They are connected to the ground by a tether and rise up thousands of feet into the air to see over the hill. With one LOROP (long-range oblique photography) system, the CA-990, developed by Eastman Kodak and Recon/Optical Inc., a general could receive images of things 200 nautical miles away taken from an 11-foot-long drone traveling at roughly 1,000 mph at 40,000 feet. He could view the images instantly or, with a laser printer, have them converted to hard copy, within seconds.

As much as the SR-71 costs to operate, and as much as its efforts can be duplicated by a spy satellite, there will always be a need for such a plane. As expensive as they are, they are still cheaper than satellites and can take pictures far faster than a satellite. As we'll see later, there are plans to build a spy plane that can go even higher and faster than the SR with even greater stealth.

5

DISCOVERER AND SAMOS—THE FIRST SPY SATELLITES

THE MISSILE PROGRAM

The great irony of the spy satellites is that they owe their development to the very thing they were put in space to spy on. The early spy satellites were boosted into orbit atop rockets that had been developed to launch nuclear weapons around the world in time of war. The stories of the spy satellite and missile program started out together, toward the end of World War II, in Germany.

Germany developed the first means for long-range, unpiloted destruction—the V-1 "buzz bomb." The V-1 was essentially a cruise missile, or drone, a mini-airplane on autopilot with a bomb on board that could hit, with reasonable accuracy, a target hundreds of miles away. The next step was to build a ballistic missile, a bomb that could be flung on an arc similar to an artillery shell, although, unlike an artillery shell, it would have its own rocket engine to propel it.

There had been some work in the field of rocketry before the German scientists turned to it in the war. More than 900 years ago the Chinese invented fireworks, building small rockets that would sail into the air and explode. Such rockets were used primarily for entertainment over the centuries. When they were used as weapons of war, they struck fear into the heart of the enemy, but did little damage and were terribly inaccurate.

In the 19th century, a Russian schoolteacher named Konstantin Tsiolkovsky did some remarkable theoretical work. One of the first to seriously connect rocketry with venturing into space, Tsiolkovsky proved through his "ideal rocket equation" that rockets would be able to maneuver even in the vacuum of space. He also theorized that rockets should be built in stages that would drop off as their fuel was consumed, a concept that was used by the space program a century later.

Other notable rocketry pioneers were Robert Goddard, the American who launched the world's first liquid-fueled rocket on March 26, 1926, and Hermann Oberth, a German schoolteacher who made enormous advances in rocketry theory.

The V-2 rockets built by the German scientists at Peenemunde on the Baltic Sea were notoriously inaccurate beasts. Like war rockets of centuries before, they were more successful in creating psychological terror than in causing effective destruction, for even over a mere 130-mile flight, a V-2 might miss its mark by up to five miles.

Indeed, the gross inaccuracy of the V-2 led many military planners in the United States to deride the very idea of long-range ballistic missiles. If a V-2, over 130 miles, was off by five miles, then a rocket traveling over 5,000 miles between continents would be off by a minimum of 20 miles. Just to be on the safe side, however, in April 1946 the Air Force awarded the Convair division of General Dynamics a small contract to study the feasibility of such missiles. That contract was canceled a year later when the Air Force decided that such missiles were the stuff of science fiction and that the future lay in long-range bombers and V-1 buzz-bomb-type cruise missiles.

The Army showed a little more interest in the idea, but they were considering shorter-range, tactical missiles, not intercontinental rockets. They sponsored a General Electric rocket research program called Project Hermes, which relied on captured German V-2 rockets and captured German V-2 scientists. Among the German scientists was Dr. Wernher von Braun, a man who would later head up America's space programs.

Project Hermes launched 67 V-2s in the White Sands, New Mexico, testing grounds between April 1946 and June 1951. Although the V-2s were huge, unpredictable behemoths, their test launches were crucial in the development of America's first ballistic missile, Redstone.

Meanwhile, the Soviets had their own cache of captured German rockets and scientists and attempted to build their own ballistic missiles. When some of those scientists were finally released, the news they brought the United States was heartening: The Soviet Union was behind America in missile research and, like the U.S. Air Force, was concentrating on cruise missiles. As it turned out, however, those German scientists had been misled. The Soviets had a separate rocket research facility that the Germans weren't privy to, and it was there that they conducted their most advanced research.

In the fall of 1952 the United States detonated its first hydrogen bomb, a far more powerful nuclear weapon than the atom bomb dropped on Hiroshima in 1945. While the American missile program had been progressing steadily (with even the previously reluctant Air Force becoming impressed with the results), the program got a real boost in 1954. The Atomic Energy Commission—the agency that built the bombs—figured out that they could make hydrogen bombs small enough to fit atop a missile.

At this point the United States assumed it was leading the missile race. That confidence began to erode when American electronic listening posts in Turkey picked up rocket-test information that told them the Soviets were doing far better than had been thought.

On January 25, 1957, the United States prepared to launch its first IRBM—intermediate-range ballistic missile—from Cape Canaveral, Florida. This huge rocket exploded on the launchpad. Meanwhile, intelligence reports indicated that the Soviets had been successfully launching two such IRBMs per month since the previous fall.

But those were only IRBMs. American missile experts were still confident that the United States led the intercontinental ballistic missile—ICBM—race. The Soviets tried to deflate that confidence in August 1957 when they announced a successful test firing of an ICBM. No one was sure whether or not to believe the Soviets.

On October 4, 1957, the U.S. officials had no choice but to believe them. On that date the Soviets launched *Sputnik 1* (*sputnik* roughly translates as "friend" or "companion"), a beachball-sized hunk of metal that became the first manmade object to be sent into orbit. If the Soviets could put something into space that could sail over the United States every 96 minutes, they could certainly launch an ICBM. *Sputnik's* little radio signal beep from orbit marked the beginning of the Space Age. It also meant the beginning, in earnest, of the nuclear missile race and, ironically, of the race to get spies in space to spy on those missiles.

FUNDAMENTALS OF SPACE

Sir Isaac Newton was the first to work out how a manmade object could be made to circle the Earth. Calculating the gravitational pull of the planet, he figured that if an object were moving fast enough (18,000 miles an hour or more) as it started to fall, the spherical surface of the Earth would always be moving out from under it. The object would, in effect, be perpetually in a state of falling. While Newton saw his object fired from a cannon on a mountaintop and not launched from a concrete pad in the middle of Central Asia, his basic principles accounted for the presence of *Sputnik* in space. In the vacuum of space, 100 miles or more above the surface, the lack of atmospheric drag would allow little *Sputnik* to keep on falling and stay in orbit.

The question is, why put something in orbit? The first to conceive of a really practical use for an orbiting object was

British scientist and science fiction writer Arthur C. Clarke. In the February 1945 issue of *Wireless World* he suggested that a satellite orbiting at 22,300 miles would be geosynchronous; it would be far enough from Earth that its 18,000 mph speed would keep it over one spot on the equator and could be used to relay communications signals to other parts of the world. Today, more than 40 years later, the communications satellite has proven to be by far the most commercially viable use of space.

Others were intrigued by the possibilities of what else could be done from orbit. A century before, in an 1869 article in the *Atlantic Monthly* called "The Brick Moon," writer Edward Everett Hale imagined an artificial Moon that could be used as a manned military station. This idea surfaced again in May 1946 when the RAND (Research and Development) Corporation (a think tank) released its Air Force-sponsored report entitled "Preliminary Design of an Experimental World-Circling Spaceship."

RAND felt that a 500-pound satellite could be put into orbit by 1951 at a cost of about $150 million. The report said there would be great military and scientific potential for such a craft, but cautioned that there was no way for anyone to predict all of the possibilities: "We can see no more clearly all the utility and implications of spaceships than the Wright brothers could see fleets of B-29s bombing Japan and air transports circling the globe. Though the crystal ball is cloudy, two things seem clear: (1) A satellite vehicle with appropriate instrumentation can be expected to be one of the most potent scientific tools of the Twentieth Century. (2) The achievement of a satellite craft by the United States would inflame the imagination of mankind, and would probably produce repercussions in the world comparable to the explosion of the atomic bomb."

There were even hints of reconnaissance capabilities: "It should also be remarked that the satellite offers an observational aircraft that cannot be brought down by an enemy who has not mastered similar techniques."

Whether because of lack of foresight, or because the idea seemed too expensive or too farfetched, the RAND report was not followed up on for eight years.

In 1954, Wernher Von Braun made a proposal to the U.S. government, stating that with the missiles already available, he could get a satellite into orbit. His proposal became Orbiter, a joint Army-Navy project. In 1955, however, it was scratched in favor of a civilian satellite project called Vanguard. That was a mistake, for Vanguard had to be created from the ground up, without the military's help. The first Vanguard launch attempt was on December 6, 1957, two months after *Sputnik*. It was a complete disaster. The rocket blew up on the launch pad, leaving the tiny satellite still bleeping amidst the debris. Someone in the control room remarked grimly, "Why doesn't someone kick it and put it out of its misery."

The Orbiter program was revitalized in a hurry and on January 31, 1958, America's first satellite, the *Explorer 1*, was launched into orbit (*Explorer* made the first scientific discovery by a satellite, detecting the Van Allen belts of highly charged particles circling the Earth at 30,000 miles).

Explorer's launch began the space race in earnest, with the Americans and the Soviets sending satellite after satellite into space. The Soviets always took the lead: Their satellites were heavier, they put the first animal into orbit, and later, the first man.

But during this time, as the two superpowers conducted this Space Age spitting contest, another space program was underway in the United States, one that the public knew nothing about.

DISCOVERER AND SAMOS

In *Across the Space Frontier*, a collection of articles on the coming space age, published in 1952, German rocket scientist and architect of the American space program Wernher von Braun wrote in his article that the great thing about a space station is that it would be "close enough to the Earth to afford a superb observation post." He outlined how it would work. "Technicians in this space station, using specially designed, powerful telescopes attached to large optical screens, radarscopes and cameras, will keep under constant inspection every ocean, continent, country and city. Even small towns will be visible...Nothing will go unobserved...Because of the telescopic eyes and cameras of the space station, it will be practically impossible for any nation to hide warlike preparations for any length of time."

RAND was thinking along the same lines as von Braun. In 1951 they put out two reports on reconnaissance satellites. The CIA was intrigued, and in 1952 it gave RAND money for a much larger and more in-depth look. In March 1954 RAND presented the CIA with a huge, two-volume study titled *An Analysis of the Potential of an Unconventional Reconnaissance Method*. The report suggested that satellites would be perfect for spying; they travel fast, covering vast areas quickly; they float silently, undisturbed by the vibrations that are the bane of aerial photography; and they couldn't, at that time, be shot down.

The CIA was *very* interested, but it knew that such a scheme would, in all likelihood, take years to get off the ground. That's why the CIA turned to the U-2 as an interim measure. While Richard Bissell became deeply engrossed in producing the U-2, he also kept alive the idea of spy satellites. He wasn't the only one interested; the Air Force was also intrigued. On March 16, 1955, the Air Force, with indirect but substantial support from the CIA, issued formal design requirements for a Strategic Satellite System, given the designation WS-117L (Weapons System-117L). Three companies were given one-year design-study contracts. On June 30, 1956, the Air Force chose Lockheed's design—called the *Agena*—and the project was given the name Pied Piper.

The *Agena* was the spacecraft that would orbit the Earth. It was to be boosted into space by an Atlas missile. The craft would be roughly 19 feet long and five feet in diameter. Most of that would be taken up by fuel and the Bell Aerospace

Hustler engine that would give it its last thrust into orbit. The nose cone of the *Agena* was replaceable, so that, theoretically, it could carry almost any payload into space. While the *Agena* has been used for some nonreconnaissance missions (it was used in the Lunar Orbiter and Canadian Alouette space shots) it was primarily designed for spying.

The big question concerned how the spying would be done. It was one thing to spy from the U-2 at 68,000 feet, but how do you do it from a 100-mile orbit, over 500,000 feet above the surface? And, while the U-2 can bring its pictures back to the ground, the satellite would be stuck in orbit.

A Lockheed Agena spacecraft, the dependable workhorse of many reconnaissance satellite missions in the 1960s. [U.S. Air Force]

The two systems considered for the Pied Piper program were television and film-scanning. The television system was straightforward: A TV camera would take pictures of the ground below, store images on tape, then beam down images when the satellite passed over an American receiving station (a ground station). Film-scanning was more complicated. The camera on board the satellite would take black-and-white photographs that would be developed on board the spacecraft. As the satellite orbited over a ground station, the photograph would be scanned by a fine beam of white light that would record the levels of black, white and gray on the photo. This information would then be translated into signals that could be beamed down by radio link.

Film-scanning posed problems. It was initially thought that beaming down the information contained in a photo would take longer than a satellite could remain over a ground station, but the resolution that television provided at the time was abysmal. Therefore, film-scanning was selected. Television would be used by the Army in its TIROS (Television and Infrared Observation System) satellites, which were originally designed for battlefield surveillance, but ended up being suited only for weather observation.

The major contractors for the film-scanning system included Eastman Kodak (various pieces of photographic equipment), CBS Laboratories (the film scanner) and Philco-Ford (signal processing and radio transmission). The most important piece of equipment, however, would be the camera and lens.

If the huge Hycon B camera used on the U-2 had been put on a satellite, the increased distance from the ground would have meant that the B camera, which could see a soldier from the U-2, would have had a hard time picking out a tank from orbit.

The answer lay in using a still bigger camera with an even longer lens. The trick to building a really long lens is to use folding optics, mirrors that bounce the image around, making it seem as if the lens were extraordinarily long. Hycon's K-30 camera had a folding optics lens with a 100-inch focal length, and Perkin Elmer built one with a 240-inch focal length. The bigger the camera, however, the greater the weight. The Hycon K-30 weighed 665 pounds. In 1958, the largest satellite the United States launched weighed 38 pounds. Nevertheless, Pied Piper continued, as confidence grew in the ability of the new, bigger boosters that were being developed to boost heavier payloads.

While this program continued, RAND came up with a startling idea. It was generally accepted that one of the drawbacks of a spy satellite, as opposed to a spy plane, was that it couldn't deliver its photos back to Earth. Why not? asked RAND. In *Physical Recovery of Satellite Payloads: A Preliminary Investigation*, RAND suggested that an ICBM nose cone, used to loft a nuclear warhead into space and protect it during its reentry into the atmosphere, could also be used to carry and reenter a photo-reconnaissance payload. The RAND plan called for a recoverable capsule, crammed with film, to disengage from the main satellite, then fire a small retrorocket to slow itself down. The capsule would then fall out of orbit, reentering the atmosphere and deploying a parachute at 50,000 feet. It would float down into the ocean, all the while transmitting a radio signal to indicate its position to the recovery team.

This rather improbable-sounding scheme did have some things in its favor: It could provide pictures of high resolution, and it could provide the PIs with actual photos, both of which the film-scanning system could not do. But it also seemed absurdly fraught with potential peril. If the capsule wasn't properly oriented when the retrorocket fired, the capsule might be knocked into a higher orbit. If it was just slightly out of whack, or if the rockets fired a moment too soon or too late, it could come down thousands of miles from where the recovery team would be waiting. Even if it did come down roughly on target, looking for it would be like walking over a football field and looking for a pea. The idea was put on the back burner.

Lack of funding and lack of real interest had kept the Air Force's spy satellite project, Pied Piper, moving slowly. *Sputnik* changed all that. Within two months, the funding for WS-117L quadrupled.

Sputnik also helped RAND's recoverable capsule reconnaissance satellite idea. Shortly after *Sputnik*, RAND
released its second report on the subject, *A Family of
Recoverable Reconnaissance Satellites*. At this point virtually
any project that had to do with space was given support. In
January 1958, the Department of Defense (DoD), with extremely vigorous support from the CIA, decided that the
recoverable-satellite concept should be tested as soon as
possible.

It was decided to try to adapt the *Agena* for a recoverable
capsule, and to boost it into orbit aboard the smaller Thor
missile, rather than wait for the larger Atlas, which was still
in production. The project was given the name Corona. To
the public it would be known as Discoverer. The public was
told that it was a scientific satellite program, embarked on
for the benefit of all mankind.

PRINCIPLES OF SPY SATELLITES

Vandenberg Air Force Base was chosen as the launch site
for spy satellites. Located on Point Arguello, 150 miles
northwest of Los Angeles, this base is the perfect spot for
launching satellites into polar orbits. To launch into a polar
orbit, a rocket must be sent up either in a northerly or
southerly direction. If a rocket was launched from Cape
Canaveral and something happened to it during the launch,
it could crash somewhere along the heavily populated east-
ern seaboard, causing an unprecedented disaster. If this
happened to a rocket launched from Vandenberg, it would
crash into the ocean.

What is a polar orbit and why do spy satellites use them?

To begin with, there are several different types of orbit and
each has its own benefit. It's important to realize that rockets
don't really go straight up. They start that way on the
launchpad, but once up, they arc off, so that when orbit is
reached, they are traveling parallel to the Earth's surface.

Many space launches, including the shuttle, are sent off in
an easterly direction. This is done, in part, to use the speed

of the Earth's rotation to help the vehicle into space. Thus, while a rocket has to go 18,000 mph to make it into orbit, if it's launched eastward it only has to go 17,000 mph; the remaining 1,000 mph is provided by the rotation of the planet. Conversely, a rocket traveling westward would have to have a speed of 19,000 mph to counter the rotational speed. Satellites launched either north or south are not affected much by the rotational speed.

One key characteristic of an orbit is its inclination, which is given in degrees. A satellite launched into the east that follows the equator has a 0-degree inclination. One launched into the north that goes directly over both poles has a 90-degree inclination. A satellite launched in a northeasterly direction could have an inclination of anywhere from 0 to 90 degrees, and one launched in a northwesterly direction could have an inclination of anywhere from 90 to 180 degrees.

Essentially, a spy satellite's orbit remains fixed; the Earth spins beneath it. The amount of ground a satellite covers is determined by its inclination. A satellite with a 0-degree inclination would only fly over the equator. A satellite with a 45-degree inclination would cover a band around the middle of the Earth, stretching from the top to the bottom of its orbit. It would only cover an area ranging from about 30 degrees north latitude (northern California) to about 30 degrees south latitude (the middle of Australia). It wouldn't cover vast areas of both the northern and southern hemispheres.

A satellite traveling directly over the poles, however, would find the entire surface of the earth spinning beneath it and, in a number of orbits, it would cover every spot on the globe. That is why most spy satellites are found in polar orbits, with orbital inclinations ranging from 90 to 110 degrees or so.

Another key characteristic of a satellite's orbit is its orbital height. The height determines the time it takes for a satellite to make one orbit. It is found that a satellite orbiting at 22,300 miles takes just as long to make one circle of the planet as it does for the planet to rotate once—24 hours. Therefore, a satellite on a 0-degree equatorial orbit, at 22,300 miles, would remain fixed over one spot on the equator—it would be geostationary, or geosynchronous. This orbit, as mentioned earlier, is used for communications satellites.

Different orbital heights are suited to different tasks. Orbits of 700 or 800 miles are often used for weather satellites as they afford a broad view of the motions of clouds below. Spy satellites characteristically like to use low orbits so that they can get a closer view of the Earth's surface. They may go as low as 70 or 80 miles. However, there is a problem with going so low. At 70 or 80 miles the satellite will encounter the outer fringe of the atmosphere and this will slow the satellite down, eventually causing it to fall out of orbit.

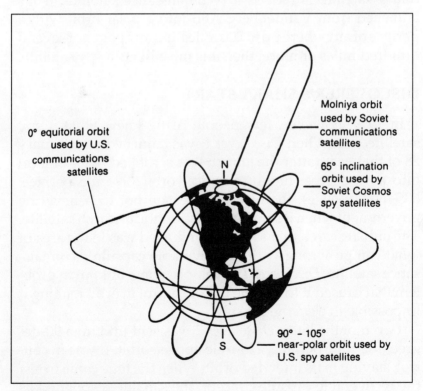

Several key orbital types.

But a satellite doesn't have to orbit continually at one altitude. Orbits are defined by their perigee—closest point to the Earth's surface—and apogee—farthest point from the surface. Satellites, such as communications satellites, that have the same apogees and perigees are on circular orbits. Satellites that have differing perigees and apogees are on elliptical orbits. Spy satellites usually follow strongly elliptical orbits, with perigees of 100 miles or less and apogees of 300 miles or more. This prolongs the orbital life of the satellite as it then spends most of its time out of the reach of the atmosphere.

When spy satellites are launched, the launches are usually conducted in relative secrecy. There's no way they can hide the actual launch itself; those rockets make a lot of noise and their rocket plumes are very bright, but the payload can be classified. There are a few clues that tip off satellite followers that a satellite is indeed a reconnaissance satellite. If it's launched from Vandenberg AFB into a polar orbit with a perigee of anywhere up to 200 miles and an apogee of several hundred miles or more, then it is most likely a spy satellite.

DISCOVERER'S SHAKY START

In 1959, however, few people really knew what a spy satellite was. When *Discoverer 1* was launched on February 28 of that year (after the launch was scrubbed twice before) into a 96-degree, highly elliptical orbit (99-mile perigee, 605-mile apogee), there was no reason not to believe the government when it said it was a scientific research satellite. The only research that satellite conducted was in the area of what can go wrong with a recoverable capsule reconnaissance satellite. *Discoverer 1* developed some unknown problem that caused it to tumble out of control in orbit making it impossible to eject the capsule.

Two months later, *Discoverer 2* was sent up into a 90-degree, 152-mile perigee, 225-mile apogee orbit. It was in control, staying in its intended orbit. When the time came to test the recoverable capsule concept, the satellite responded as it was supposed to. Gas jets were used to maneuver the *Agena* spacecraft so that it was angled down. When the retrorockets were fired the capsule would be driven down into the atmosphere. Everything was fine up until then. But the retrorockets fired prematurely and the capsule reentered the atmosphere too soon. It was to have come down somewhere near Hawaii. Instead, it was last sighted somewhere over the northern tip of Norway. It was never recovered, at least not by the United States; some think the Soviets picked it up.

Discoverer was having trouble. It only got worse. Of the next eight Discoverers, four didn't even make it into orbit, one made it into orbit but tumbled out of control, and three reentered capsules that were never recovered. Some design changes were made for *Discoverer 11*: It would eject tiny strands of foil that would make its descent easier to pick up on radar. But *Discoverer 11* was not spotted in the recovery area.

Time to go back to the drawing boards. The satellites were sent to an independent engineering test facility in Tennessee. There was a certain amount of relief when the problem was discovered: The retrorockets, after prolonged exposure to the extreme cold of space, could misfire and, in addition, something was wrong with the way the capsule's parachute deployed. So changes were made and incorporated into *Discoverer 12*.

Discoverer 12, launched June 29, 1960, failed to enter into orbit.

President Eisenhower, who had been promised an operating spy satellite system by the spring of 1959, was not pleased and expressed his anger to Dulles and Bissell. Bissell, in turn, was simply furious with the technology. A quote from Bissell in Ray Cline's *Secrets, Spies and Scholars* summed it up: "It was a most heartbreaking business. If an airplane goes on a test flight and something malfunctions, and it gets back, the pilot can tell you something about the malfunction, or you can look it over and find out. But in the case of a recce

Discoverer 13 *launched from Vandenberg Air Force Base. [U.S. Air Force]*

[reconnaissance] satellite, you fire the damn thing off, and you've got some telemetry [the signals sent to and from a satellite to monitor and operate it], and you never get it back. There is no pilot, of course, and you've got no hardware. You never see it again. So you have to infer from telemetry what went wrong. Then you make a fix and if it fails again, you know you've inferred wrong. In the case of Corona [Discoverer] it went on and on."

It was suggested that, due to superstition, *Discoverer 13* should be given the number 14. However superstition was set aside, and on August 10, 1960, number 13 was launched into a 153-mile perigee, 375-mile apogee, 93-degree orbit. The flight was monitored by the Satellite Test Control Center in Sunnyvale, California. As far as they could see, number 13 was working as planned. The spacecraft was oriented to eject the capsule, and as the satellite came over the North Pole on its 17th orbit, Sunnyvale notified the ground station in Kodiak, Alaska, to send the reentry signal to the satellite.

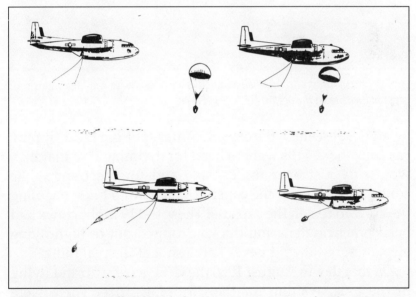

Air Force diagram illustrating the air-recovery concept for the Discoverer program. [U.S. Air Force]

Kodiak signaled for ejection. The capsule retrofired on schedule and reentered the atmosphere, deploying its parachute at 50,000 feet as planned. Now came another tricky part of the operation.

The plan called for the satellite to be picked out of the air before it hit the ocean. To do this, C-119 cargo planes were outfitted with a special trapeze harness contraption. These planes were sent into the air over the target recovery area to

A Navy diver jumps from a helicopter to secure cables to the Discoverer 13 *capsule floating in the ocean. [U.S. Air Force]*

await the descent of the capsule. After spotting the dropping capsule, the C-119s were to head for it, timing it so that they would fly just over the capsule and for the trapeze-like contraption to snag the capsule's parachute lines, enabling the crew to reel in the capsule. These C-119 flight crews had been practicing snaring things dropped out of high-flying airplanes, but they'd never had a shot at the real thing.

On that day in August 1960 the C-119s were up and flying in the area, waiting for the dropping prize. There were surface ships below in case they should miss it. They did miss it (there was heavy cloud cover at 10,000 feet), but they did catch sight of it as it stabbed through the clouds. At least they had a good idea where it came down. They spotted the capsule in the water from the air and, within hours, a ship was alongside. Divers jumped in, secured the capsule to lines, and it was hauled up into the hovering helicopter. This was the first man-made object to be recovered from space.

Discoverer was a public program and a good deal of coverage was given to fishing the capsule out of the sea.

Eisenhower, in a public announcement, went so far as to say that it demonstrated that the United States "leads the world in the activities in the space field that promise real benefits to mankind." The Soviets didn't quite agree. They had a good idea what Discoverer was really up to, and scorned the American space program as "espionage" in a bulletin put out by the U.S.S.R. Academy of Sciences. At that point, though, Discoverer was still just being tested and there probably weren't any sensors on board.

Discoverer 14 went up eight days later. Like its predecessor, its orbit was on target and it reentered the capsule into the atmosphere flawlessly. The C-119s received the first strong signal shortly after 8:00 A.M. Captain Harold E. Mitchell was in command of the C-119 closest to the dropping target. His crew spotted the capsule, and he headed for it.

Even attached to the parachute, the capsule was dropping at about 25 feet per second. Timing was crucial. With the trapeze trailing behind, the plane came in, just missing, the trapeze almost grazing the top of the parachute. The plane made a second pass, this time missing by several feet. There was time for one last attempt before the capsule hit the cloud layer at 7,500 feet and disappeared. This time Captain Mitchell skimmed the plane just over the plummeting parachute canopy, the trapeze neatly catching up the parachute lines, securing the capsule. There were cheers inside the C-119, and later, cheers in Washington. Discoverer was ready for work.

SAMOS

Even though all the attention was focused on Discoverer, the Air Force had not lost interest in WS-117L, or Pied Piper, the film-scan/radio-transmission method for satellite reconnaissance. In early September 1960 it was given a new name—SAMOS, for Satellite and Missile Observation System. It was the only American spy satellite program ever publicly acknowledged to be a spy satellite program. Al-

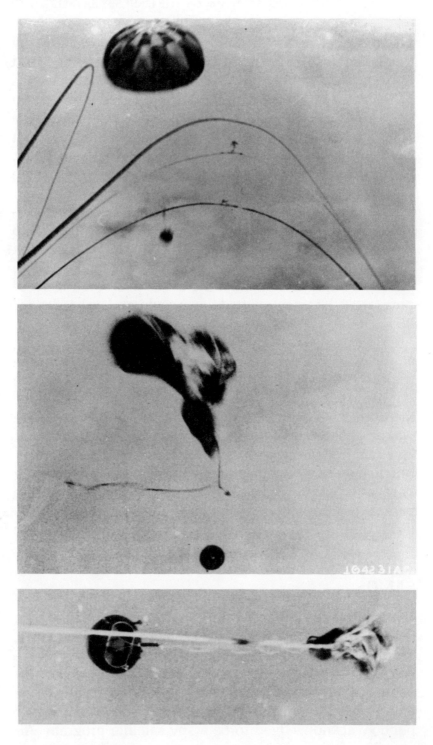

The Discoverer 14 *capsule as trapeze snags the parachute lines and the capsule is hauled aboard. (U.S. Air Force)*

though its existence was, for a brief time, a matter of public record, control of the operation was given to the new top-secret organization Eisenhower created to run the spy satellites, the National Reconnaissance Office.

The first launch of a SAMOS satellite was attempted a few months after the first Discoverer successes. Unfortunately, that first launch on October 11, 1960, was more reminiscent of the early Discoverer failures than the later successes. A cable failed to disconnect during the launch, ripping off part of the satellite. *SAMOS 2*, however, launched January 31, 1961, made it into its intended orbit.

Discoverer may have been the first American spy satellite to make it into orbit, but SAMOS was the first to do real spying. Even if *Discoverers 14* and *15* had been carrying cameras, because of the size of the Agena and the weight restrictions imposed by the heavy reentry capsule, they couldn't have taken up large cameras and the pictures taken would not have had high resolution. *SAMOS 2*, however, was fully operational the moment it reached orbit.

What could *SAMOS 2* see? If the camera on board had a focal length of only 40 inches (a relatively small Perkin Elmer would have done the trick) and film that could resolve 100 lines per millimeter, the satellite from its orbit could then have been able to spot objects as small as 20 feet across on the ground. This resolution would have been enough to turn up the 100-foot-long missiles and related facilities that were the most pressing intelligence target of the time.

The cameras on *SAMOS 2* could photograph an area 50 miles by 50 miles, needing only 4,000 photos to cover the entire Soviet Union and only 1,000 photos for areas deemed to be of strategic interest. The satellite was only operational for about a month, during which time it completed 500 orbits. When it was no longer useful, after running out of film, it would be de-orbited and allowed to burn up in the atmosphere.

While it had been operational, *SAMOS 2* likely did what was required of it—observe missiles. Estimates based on U-2 photos put Soviet ICBM strength at about 120 missiles. The photos taken by *SAMOS 2* cut this estimate in half to 60 missiles. This figure would continue to drop. In late 1959 it had been estimated that the Soviets would have 400 ICBMs by the summer of 1961. Yet when photo interpreters scoured more photos in September 1961, they found that rather than having 400 such missiles to launch at the United States, the Soviets had 14.

The U-2 brought back the first indications that the missile gap was an illusion. The early spy satellites gave evidence that the missile gap did in fact exist; it was just that it was decidedly in favor of the United States.

Not all the spying was done by SAMOS. With *Discoverers 16* and *17*, a new, larger *Agena* was used, and *Discoverer 18* saw the first use of a larger booster. This meant that larger payloads (i.e., larger cameras) could be sent into space. Because there weren't the limits on resolution posed by the film-scan/radio-transmission technique, these Discoverers could take photos with remarkably high resolution. It is estimated that these Discoverers, from 100 miles up, could pick out objects as small as a foot across. Bissell was later quoted in *Deep Black* as saying that these early photos were "very, very good," and that the photo interpreters "were now so good that they were able to identify the make of almost every car in Red Square from the photography."

There were worldwide, history-making consequences to these early photographs. Khrushchev planned on using the missile gap to get his way in Berlin in 1961. Berlin is a city divided between East and West, with an actual wall crowned with barbed wire separating the part of the city that is run by communist East Germany from the part that is governed by West Germany. Khrushchev tried to use the missile gap to pry the remainder of Berlin from the West. The United States stood steadfastly against this, but was unnerved. Could this stalemate lead to a confrontation between the two superpowers, perhaps *the* confrontation, nuclear war?

In October 1961 there was a change in the stalemate. The United States remained committed to keeping part of Berlin in the West, but the Americans no longer seemed so concerned with the Soviet threat. Even more surprisingly, the Soviet position weakened and Khrushchev backed off. Why such a change?

On October 6, 1961, President Kennedy returned from a family vacation for a meeting with Soviet Foreign Minister Andrei Gromyko. He then told Gromyko that the missile gap existed, but that it was in America's favor, not the Soviet Union's. And he had proof. He showed Gromyko photographs of Soviet missile bases, taken from orbit. Caught in their lie, the Soviets had no choice but to back down.

There were other consequences, however. Whenever an intelligence source is revealed to an enemy, it is compromised, even if it is a spy satellite. It was feared that the

Soviets, with their noses rubbed in cold evidence of satellite spying, would try to knock the satellites out of orbit. There was also the fear that the Soviet Union would bury the United States in a far less expensive, but no less effective way—politically. If they announced to the world the existence of the satellites and equated them with the U-2, they might get the United States to terminate them. The question was, what did the Soviets think of spying from space?

The United States took the view that satellites of any kind, spy or otherwise, did not violate a nation's airspace. They saw space as something beyond a nation's jurisdiction, comparable to the open seas. The Soviets could have taken the opposing view, and to a certain extent they did. But there were also other signals that seemed to indicate that the Soviets were indifferent to the idea. In *Waging Peace: 1956-1961*, Eisenhower recalled a relevant comment Khrushchev made at the Paris summit conference after the U-2 incident. When de Gaulle questioned Khrushchev about Soviet satellites flying over France, "Khrushchev broke in to say he was talking about airplanes, not about satellites. He said any nation in the world who wanted to photograph the Soviet areas by satellite was completely free to do so."

But Khrushchev's off-the-cuff remarks could not be taken as statements of official policy. There were other statements that pointed in the other direction. An editorial in the *Red Star* (the Soviet armed forces newspaper) of July 23, 1961, exclaimed that "A spy is a spy, no matter what height it flies." Later, during negotiations concerning the peaceful uses of space, the Soviets made an official demand to ban spy satellites.

It was in this atmosphere of uncertainty over just what the Soviets would do in response to spy satellites that Kennedy opted to terminate the spy satellite programs—at least officially. After *SAMOS 3* exploded on the launchpad on September 9, 1961, the SAMOS program came to an abrupt end. Discoverer, a widely-hailed public program with a good cover as a scientific satellite didn't have to be halted so quickly. The remaining launches were carried out, with an overall success rate of better than 50%, all the way up through *Discoverer 31*. After that there were no more Discoverers.

But of course the spy satellite programs did not end, they just got coats of paint and new names. They both were painted *black*; they became top secret. The whole spy satellite program for overhead reconnaissance was given the appropriately wry name of Keyhole (as in spying through a keyhole), and every type of satellite was given a KH (keyhole) number. Retroactively, a SAMOS satellite became a KH-1 and a Discoverer was a KH-4 (no one is really sure what happened to KH-2 and KH-3).

As it turned out, the Soviets were not all that upset about spy satellites. They made the necessary complaints and shouts in an attempt to harass the United States. But they weren't able to mount an all-out war, for the simple reason that they were developing their own spy satellites as fast as possible. In 1963 they ceased complaining, publicly and privately, about American spy satellites, for it was in that year that they launched their own.

In May 1964 Khrushchev was interviewed in Moscow by Senator William Benson. According to Benson, the Soviet premier requested that U-2 flights over Cuba be halted. He said that satellites were adequate and less provocative. "If you wish," said Khrushchev to Benson, "I can show you photos of your military bases taken from outer space. I will show them to President Johnson, if he wishes." Then, joking even further, "Why don't we exchange such photos?"

What Khrushchev jokingly suggested was, in fact, essentially what Eisenhower had put forward in 1956 in his Open Skies proposal. Since then there has been a tacit understanding between the two superpowers that spy satellites are acceptable, that they benefit both sides by helping to create stability.

But the United States did not want the Soviets to achieve equality in the spy satellite arena. The Americans had launched the first successful reconnaissance satellites and had a technological lead in the field. The United States wanted to maintain that lead. The only way to keep ahead in the race was build bigger and better spy satellites.

6

BIGGER AND BETTER SPIES

While the Air Force actually launched both the SAMOS and Discoverer satellites, it didn't sponsor both programs. Discoverer was really the CIA's program—it had backed the recoverable capsule concept from the RAND reports on—while the Air Force was more fully involved in the film-scan/radio-transmission concept of SAMOS. The rivalry that had arisen between the two agencies over the U-2 continued over the satellites. That was the main reason President Eisenhower created the National Reconnaissance Office (NRO) to stop the bickering, infighting and back-stabbing.

He wanted the spy satellite programs to be coordinated by a third party. Although the NRO is part of Air Force intelligence, it is a civilian operation; its chief is the under-secretary of the Air Force, and the second in command is appointed from the CIA.

The NRO supposedly had control over the entire spy satellite program, but, in fact, there continued to be two separate programs. The Air Force concentrated on SAMOS-like satellites that used the film-scan/radio-transmission concept. Because these satellites couldn't take pictures with the same high resolution of the Discoverer satellites, they became known as *area-survey* satellites; they would cover the bigger picture. They were given the designation KH-5.

After two launch failures, the first KH-5 made it into orbit on May 18, 1963. Six more launches came that year, and in 1964 and 1965, an average of about one per month was lofted into space. The KH-5s would stay in orbit for three to four weeks, which basically gave the United States almost continuous overhead coverage of the Soviet Union. Their launches were timed so that on each pass the satellites would cross over Russia a little after midday. This is called a Sun-synchronous orbit: In every picture taken, the sunlight was at the same angle, causing tall objects to cast similar shadows day after day. That way it was easy to detect changes.

The KH-5s could spot something on the ground that was seven feet or more across. This resolution couldn't approach what the Discoverer-type satellites could produce, but it was sufficient to be able to spot missiles. The first fruits of the KH-5 were the discoveries that the Soviets were building their own Polaris-type submarines and that they were digging silos for their new generations of ICBMs.

The recoverable capsule successors to Discoverer were known as *close-look* satellites because they were able to use lower orbits and take pictures of higher resolution. They were given the designation KH-6. The first of these were launched in 1962. Because of their low orbit, they would only stay in orbit for three or four days. These were designed to be situational, occasional-use satellites. The KH-5 area-survey satellites would be up in orbit almost continuously, transmitting their reasonably good photos to Earth. When a need arose for pictures of higher resolution, a KH-6 close-look could be sent up to take a quick peek.

Neither the KH-5 nor the KH-6 was a significant improvement on its predecessor. In effect, both SAMOS and Discoverer were test programs and the KH-5 and KH-6 were the first fully operational area-survey and close-look satellite programs. Bigger advances would come with the KH-7 area-survey and KH-8 close-look satellites that were put into orbit in 1966.

The first of the third generation of spy satellites to fly was a KH-8 close-look, launched on July 29, 1966. As progressively larger booster rockets were developed, ever larger payloads could be put into orbit. No longer using Thors or Atlases, the KH-8 was lofted up atop a huge Titan 3B, which could put a 6,000-pound payload into space. The most revolutionary part of this payload—housed in the new, larger Agena-D—was that it had *two* recoverable film-pack capsules. The combination of having that much more film on board and the use of a slightly higher orbit (which would have less atmospheric drag) meant that the KH-8 could stay in orbit longer than its predecessor. While the KH-6s were limited to three to five days in orbit, the KH-8 started with an orbital life of eight days, increasing to 15 days per mission by 1968.

Improvements were also made in the reconnaissance equipment. For the first time a multispectral camera, built by Itek, was put on board. This camera photographed in six different bandwidths of light. The reason this is useful is that objects reflect the various bandwidths in different ways. For example, on film that registers light from all bandwidths together, a newly mowed lawn and a lawn that hasn't been cut for weeks would both look green. If both these lawns were photographed only in the red spectrum, the newly mowed lawn would reflect more light and appear to be lighter in color than the uncut grass. Other parts of the spectrum—yellow, blue, orange, green, etc.—could be used to show other differences.

The first KH-7 third-generation area-survey satellite also went up that summer, on August 9. It used a bigger and more powerful Thor rocket as its booster, one that could put 20% larger payloads into orbit.

The KH-7 showed several improvements over the KH-5. It was the first to use infrared (IR) sensors. IR sensors picked up light that falls below red on the visible part of the spectrum, and that includes thermal radiation, or heat. IR sensors can be used to take pictures of things in the dark, solely from the heat they produce. Although the IR sensors put on board the KH-7s undoubtedly produced images of relatively poor quality, they were, nonetheless, the first pictures of the Earth taken at night.

Two other important improvements that were made with the KH-7 concerned the problem of getting the images to the ground as fast as possible. The slowest part of the process was the transmission stage, when the photos were beamed to Earth. With the SLGS (Space Link Ground System) this transmission time was drastically reduced. The other development was the use of communications satellites to relay the information to Washington. With the previous generation of area-survey satellites, images would be beamed down to the nearest ground station and stored on magnetic tape. That tape would then be flown to Washington so that the photographs could be looked at. Using communications satellites eliminated that intermediary step of flying the tape to the United States; the information could be sent there directly.

FLESH-AND-BLOOD SPIES IN SPACE?

While the Air Force and the CIA were launching secret spy satellites into space from Vandenberg AFB in California, the world's attention was focused on Florida, where NASA was launching its own rockets. While the payloads in the Air Force and CIA launches were usually cameras, NASA's most coveted payloads were human beings.

At that point the manned missions were all purely civilian ventures, part of President Kennedy's goal to put a man on the Moon and return him safely to Earth by the end of the 1960s. But what about espionage missions in space? What about putting real human spies into orbit?

There is one simple reason why the idea hadn't yet been explored: Putting men into space—and getting them back to Earth safely—is frighteningly expensive. The cameras in a spy satellite don't need to eat or breathe, and the cost of providing such expendables is astronomical. On the other hand, there would be benefits to putting a "James Bond" in orbit.

There are two major problems with unmanned reconnaissance satellites. First, they don't always get the pictures you want, and you don't know if they are missing something important. In some of the early American manned flights, humans could see objects on the surface far better than had been expected. It had been thought astronauts would only be able to see things 200 feet across or larger. But astronauts in the Mercury program in 1963 said that they could easily spot large landmarks, and astronaut Gordon Cooper said he could pick out individual houses and streets when he flew over Tibet. If that's what could be seen with the unaided eye, then the idea of what they could see with high-powered binoculars and telescopes was tantalizing. Human spies in space wouldn't have to do all the reconnaissance themselves, but they could spot targets and point cameras.

The second problem with unmanned reconnaissance satellites is that if they break down in space, no one can do anything about it. Having astronauts in space to repair broken reconnaissance equipment was extremely enticing. The combination of using humans to spot objects and point cameras and also using them as repairmen prompted the Pentagon to announce, on January 23, 1965, that it had approved studies for a Manned Orbiting Laboratory—MOL (pronounced "mole").

To test the idea of flesh-and-blood spies in space, the astronauts on the *Gemini 4* and *5* missions were given cameras. The pictures, given that the camera lenses were rather small, showed remarkable resolution. In one picture taken of an airfield outside Dallas, buildings and runways can be easily spotted. On August 25, 1965, the Soviet military newspaper *Red Star* accused the *Gemini 5* astronauts of spying. That same day, President Lyndon Johnson gave the go-ahead to build MOL.

It was estimated to cost $1.5 billion to build and launch the first five MOLs. Each one was to weigh 25,000 pounds,

An artist's conception of the aborted Manned Orbiting Laboratory, with Gemini capsule attached. [U.S. Air Force]

with 5,000 pounds devoted solely to the reconnaissance equipment. The rest of the weight would be taken up by the structure and the life-support and subsidiary systems. The design for the MOL itself made it look simply like a huge, elongated soda can, with a Gemini capsule fixed to one end. That capsule was to have been used by the astronauts to get back to Earth at the end of a mission. Initially, each mission was to last only one month. Later missions would be designed to last longer; replacement crews would come up in Gemini capsules that the retiring crew would use to return home. The last crew would use the capsule built in the MOL to return.

MOL was in trouble right from the beginning. First there was the never-ending CIA vs. Air Force jurisdictional dispute. The CIA argued that as a manned spying mission, like the U-2 missions, MOL should be theirs. The Air Force argued that the manned military mission they would be launching should come under their control. President Johnson sided with the Air Force, telling the CIA that it would have to share the project.

The biggest problem with MOL was whether or not it was worth it. Proponents of MOL touted the importance of having astronauts man the reconnaissance equipment and fix it when necessary. Detractors answered, "That's it? Billions of dollars to put repairmen in space?" By many calculations it would cost more to put up astronauts as repairmen than it would to launch several expendable spy satellites.

The cost factor weighed ever heavier on MOL as time passed and the MOL itself became heavier and slower. Within a year its proposed weight had ballooned to 30,000 pounds—more weight, more money—and the first launch was pushed back from 1968 to 1969 and eventually to 1970. And the projected cost kept growing as well: $1.5 billion became $2.2 billion, and finally $3 billion. The United States was, at that time, involved in another costly military venture, the war in Vietnam. Anything viewed as possibly extraneous or of questionable value was cut loose. In June 1969, President Richard Nixon's secretary of defense, Melvin Laird, announced the cancellation of MOL. By that point $1.62 billion had already been spent on it (more than its original projected cost) and there was little to show for it. By comparison, the total cost of the first generation of spy satellites was $1.5 billion.

MOL was to have been the ultimate spy satellite of its day. It had even been given its own Keyhole designation—KH-10. Usually when a major military program is canceled there is an uproar from interested parties, saying that national security will be threatened. Not this time. The intelligence

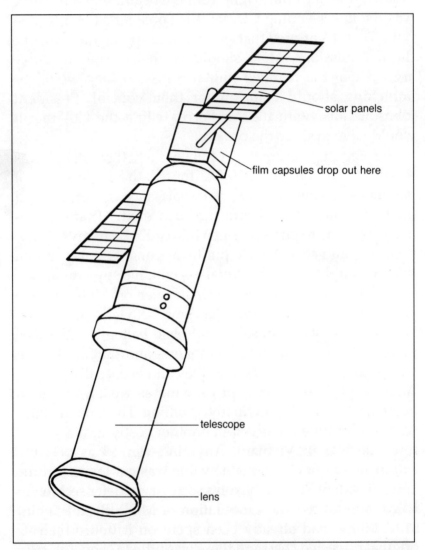

An artist's conception of the Big Bird reconnaissance satellite. Much of its length is taken up by the huge telescope. The recoverable capsules would be released from the end with the large solar panels. [U.S. Air Force]

community wasn't worried. The third-generation KH-7 and KH-8 spy satellites were doing the job, and there was another spy satellite in the works. Given the designation KH-9, it had been on the drawing board before MOL, and its designers fully believed that when this "Big Bird" flew, there would be no need for flesh-and-blood spies in space.

BIG BIRD

The only thing better than having successful area-survey satellites and successful close-look satellites would have been a combination of the two satellites. That's what Big Bird, the KH-9, was. Nicknamed Big Bird because of its enormous size, its protective launch shroud was 50 feet long and 10 feet wide and it weighed 29,000 pounds. A Big Bird on top of its Titan 3D booster stood over 17 stories high on the launchpad.

In combining the area-survey and close-look missions, Big Bird had both a film-scan/radio-transmission package on board, and four recoverable capsules that could take film back to Earth. Along with this, Big Bird is also reported to have had a high- resolution television camera on board that could quickly scan to spot areas and guide the bigger cameras. The main lens on Big Bird employed a huge mirror, six feet across, that would reflect images onto a second mirror, which could be angled to direct the image to any of the sensing packages, such as the multispectral camera or the IR sensor. Big Bird may also have been the first camera to be quipped with synthetic or side-locking aperture radar (SLAR), which can form images with radar, allowing the satellite to see through clouds and at night.

The first of two test missions for Big Bird was launched June 15, 1971. Big Bird became operational with its third launch, July 7, 1972. The satellite was sent up into a 100-mile perigee, 170-mile apogee, 96-degree inclination orbit—the characteristic spy satellite orbit. Remarkably, however, even at such a relatively low orbit, a Big Bird could remain up for up to six months. It was able do this because much of its weight was taken up by fuel, which was used to maneuver the satellite in orbit, boosting it when the atmosphere slowed it down. This maneuverability also allowed it to revisit an area day after day, instead of having its ground track slowly shift as happens with an unmaneuverable satellite.

At the end of a mission, after all its capsules had been sent back to Earth and it had run out of film, a Big Bird was exploded in orbit. The fear was that it was so huge that part of it might survive reentering the atmosphere and crash into the Earth. The worry was not only that people might get hurt, but that the satellite fragment might be recovered by the Soviets.

Big Birds were launched at a rate of roughly two per year from 1972 through 1976, and then only one (or none) a year until 1983 when, for all intents and purposes, the program came to an end. Big Bird was a culmination of the area-survey and close-look satellite programs that began with SAMOS and Discoverer. The satellite that took over from Big Bird is something different altogether. It does things that its predecessors only dreamed of and it is extraordinarily expensive (running $1 billion over budget just to get it operational). It is the KH-11.

7

THE KH-11

Something strange happened around the middle of December 1976. What was at first thought to be another Big Bird was launched from Vandenberg AFB into a 153-mile perigee, 331-mile apogee orbit. Stranger still, after four days this spacecraft was boosted into a still higher orbit, only to be lowered three months later. Even stranger, as time passed it became apparent that this was no ordinary Big Bird, staying in orbit long beyond a Big Bird's normal six-month limit.

The first inkling of this spacecraft's true identity reached the public in 1978 when a government employee, William P. Kampiles, was tried and convicted for selling a spy satellite manual to the Soviets. The satellite in question was only identified as the KH-11. This then was the newest generation of American spy satellite.

Outwardly a KH-11 resembles a Big Bird; it, too, is the size and weight of a boxcar (64 feet long, 10 feet wide, weighing roughly 30,000 pounds). And, like a Big Bird, it has been shown to be capable of extensive maneuvering in orbit. But there is one significant difference between a KH-11 and a Big Bird, and all previous spy satellites for that matter. The KH-11 doesn't have any film on board.

The KH-11 uses a digital imaging sensing system. As with a Big Bird, light is magnified and focused by a huge telescope; using folding optics, the telescope can have a focal length of approximately 20 feet. But whereas a Big Bird's telescope would focus this light onto a sheet of film, the KH-11 telescope puts the image down on an optical plane that is a field of tiny sensors, miniature light detectors that sense the level of light striking them.

This works something like the retina in the human eye, which is a carpet of detectors known as rods and cones. When a rod or cone is struck by light, it sends a signal to the brain, and the brain fuses the information from all the rods and cones into one picture. Similarly, the KH-11 can bring together the information gathered by its tiny sensors. One difference though: While the human brain forms a color picture of what the eyes see, the KH-11 only sees in black and white, or, to be more precise, various levels of gray, over 1,000 separate shades of gray.

Each light-sensitive detector corresponds to one picture element, or *pixel*. If you've ever looked closely at a TV screen (not great for your eyes) you'll have seen that it's a field of dots, which, when you stand at a distance, all come together to form one picture. Each one of those dots is a pixel. Each pixel in a KH-11, when struck by light, is assigned a digital value that represents that location of the pixel and the level of light striking it. In order to get the kind of resolution that it needs, the KH-11 has to have an extraordinary number of pixels jammed onto the optical plane, perhaps a *billion* or more.

These digital values can be beamed to another spot and used to reconstruct the image. As the images are constantly changing as the KH-11 flies over the Earth, the picture moves. The images the KH-11 gathers can be watched on a very high resolution video monitor, or they can be "frozen" and reproduced in even higher resolution photographs.

While the KH-11 "sees" in black and white, it can be difficult for the human eye to discern the difference between finely graded levels of gray. Therefore, the various levels are assigned colors, almost arbitrarily. That's why the KH-11 and similar remote-sensing satellites, like the civilian

Landsats, produce what are called "false color" images. In one of these images, vegetation may come out red, snow blue and water yellow.

One of the most revolutionary aspects of the KH-11 is its mirror. A major problem with spying from space is that the atmosphere affects the path of the light bouncing up off the Earth's surface, distorting the images that a reconnaissance satellite collects. These perturbations in the atmosphere were predicted and accounted for in the images taken from previous satellites, but the KH-11 was the first to do something about them. The KH-11 employs a "rubber mirror"; the main mirror in the telescope is made out of thin, flexible material that can be manipulated and adjusted to negate the effects of the atmosphere.

Another key development with the KH-11 is its use of a photomultiplier. Previous satellites had IR sensing systems that could be used to see at night by detecting the invisible radiation that objects give off in the form of heat. A photomultiplier, however, uses available light in the visible spectrum and multiplies it tens of thousands of times until an image is visible. Photomultipliers are used in night-vision devices on Earth, primarily by the military and law enforcement personnel to see at night. With a photomultiplier, a KH-11 would be able to see objects under starlight as clearly as if they were under direct sunlight.

The KH-11 has also brought the intelligence community one step closer to one of its ultimate goals—"real time" satellite imagery. The desire is to see things on the ground as they are happening. With the old recoverable capsule close-look spy satellites, weeks might pass before a photograph taken in space was brought to Earth, developed and analyzed. With the film-scan/radio-transmission satellites, days might pass between the time a picture was taken and it made its way to Washington for interpretation. With the KH-11, it is a question of hours at most, sometimes only minutes. The digital information is relayed through space by other satellites and is picked up on the ground at Fort

Belvoir in Virginia. The only delay comes in signal transmission and processing; a billion pixels of information, changing every second, makes for a lot of information to send.

The question that most people want answered about the KH-11 is, How good is it? What can it really see?

Whenever there is a mention of spy satellites in the press, there is usually some reference to the report that they can read license plate numbers from outer space. There are also stories that spy satellites can tell heads from tails on a 50-cent piece laying on the ground; that there is a spy satellite photo of a man in Siberia reading an issue of *Pravda* (the national Soviet newspaper) and that one can make out the headline; and that they can tell the sex of a cat. Former director of the Central Intelligence Agency, Stansfield Turner, was quoted in the February 6, 1978, issue of *Newsweek* as saying that an American spy satellite could tell the difference between a Guernsey and Hereford cow.

These claims, even if true, don't necessarily say much about the KH-11's resolving power. The sex of a cat and the breed of a cow could be indicated by their size. No satellite could read a newspaper from space or tell heads from tails. But *Pravda*, by its own specific layout and ratio between black ink and white page, would have a spectral signature that is different from any other newspaper. Similarly, the sides of a coin might also be distinguished. As for reading license plates from space, in an interview with the author, former senior CIA officer Victor Marchetti said such claims are "pure unadulterated [expletive deleted]."

To read a license plate from space, a KH-11 would have to have a ground resolution of a half inch or less. It doesn't have that. The KH-11 probably has a resolving power in the two- to four-inch range; it could pick out a license plate from space, but it sure couldn't read it. The CIA, of course, isn't going to correct anyone for saying such things. They're not about to give the Soviets any help in figuring out what the satellite can and cannot do.

The KH-11 really doesn't need to have better resolution than that. It can do so many other things that resolution, after a point, almost becomes secondary. The most revolutionary aspect of the KH-11 is that the information it provides is digital—it's all numbers. The combination of computers and the KH-11's digital information has done amazing things for the science of photo interpretation.

PIs can now see facilities and objects in three dimensions. Whether it's a nuclear-powered aircraft carrier being constructed at a Nikolaiev shipyard on the Baltic Sea, or a missile complex in the Ural mountains, the KH-11 can take successive pictures of the object of interest from several different angles. A computer takes that information and constructs, on a high-resolution video screen, a three-dimensional image that the PI is able to manipulate.

What's more, the computer can take over the most time-consuming tasks of the PI. As mentioned earlier, a PI will concentrate on one area or one facility, looking for changes. Now a computer can compare a picture taken of the shipyard this week with one taken four months ago to see how construction of the carrier is proceeding. The PI can also use the computer to search photos for particular patterns and shapes. Computers can even do much of the basic photo interpretation, scanning photographs for things that merit a closer look.

With all these great things said about the KH-11, it should be noted that not everyone is happy with it. In an interview, Victor Marchetti, a former officer of the CIA and noted critic of the agency, expressed the opinion that it collected too much information. "More and more collection does not necessarily increase the quality of your information. Photographs of an installation taken every minute are probably worth no more than a photograph taken every week. But there is that temptation—'We can get a picture every minute!'—that appeals to the moneyspenders in the Pentagon. It's so dazzling it's hard to resist. We have to be careful. There is a tendency to collect more and more of the same information, and it becomes superfluous."

Most critics of the KH-11, however, aren't concerned that it's providing America with too much intelligence, but too little. When American intelligence analysts first figured out that the huge facility being built at Abalakova in Siberia was a radar station for antiballistic missiles, they didn't use the KH-11 to get more pictures. They sent up one of the last close-look KH-8s to get photographs of the highest possible resolution. The fact that the KH-11 isn't up to all tasks annoys its critics. And what bothers the critics even more is that because of the KH-11, there aren't any other satellites left that can do the other jobs.

The problem is money. Reports have it that the KH-11 went about $1 billion over budget before it even flew. It cost so much that it drained money out of the other spy satellite programs. With the KH-11 being built there was no room for anymore Big Birds or KH-8s. Interestingly, critics of the KH-11 came predominantly from within the Air Force, while its sponsor was the CIA. The Air Force felt that it would have been better to keep the close-look recoverable-capsule satellite program going rather than dump everything into the KH-11. The irony here is that when the spy satellite programs began, it was the CIA that supported the close-look program and the Air Force that dismissed it.

In the case of the KH-11, it appears that the Air Force was right. Concentrating all of America's spy satellite resources on just one satellite has limited the flexibility of America's overhead reconnaissance capability. Although the plan was to always have two KH-11s in orbit at any one time, it didn't always work out that way. Critics said building the KH-11 at the expense of the other satellites put all of America's reconnaissance eggs in one basket. They felt it could threaten America's intelligence capability and, therefore, its security. As we will see in a later chapter of this book, they were right.

8

OTHER MILITARY SATELLITES

The KH-11 isn't the only American military satellite in orbit. It isn't even the only American spy satellite in orbit, for other kinds of spying involve more than just taking pictures. Electronic intelligence (or ELINT) satellites eavesdrop on communications, radar transmissions and missile tests; early-warning satellites detect missile launches; Navy spy satellites monitor ocean traffic. There are also communications satellites, data-relay satellites and navigation satellites, all owned and operated by the Department of Defense.

EARLY-WARNING SATELLITES

The string of lonely outposts across the American and Canadian arctic that form the DEW (distant early warning) line were built in the 1950s to warn the United States of a surprise Soviet bomber attack. When the Soviets unveiled their new swept-wing, 600-mph Backfire bomber in 1954, the DEW line's four-hour warning was cut back to two hours. When the Soviets announced their first successful test of an ICBM in 1975, the DEW line warning was obliterated; the lonely radar posts couldn't pick up a missile warhead hurtling down out of space at 5,000 mph.

Another alarm system was need to replace the DEW line, and so, for $800 million, two massive radar stations, one in

A DEW line station in the Canadian arctic. [U.S. Air Force]

Greenland and the other in Alaska, were built in 1958. This BMEWS (ballistic missile early warning system) could provide 15-minute notice of a missile attack, enough time for a president to launch a counterattack, but not enough time to confirm that the warning was real. A president would be put in the horrifying position of having to decide whether or not to launch what could turn out to be an unprovoked nuclear attack. More time was needed. Work began on a new system that would provide 30-minutes' warning; something could pick up a launch shortly after it occurred. Unlike the DEW line or BMEWS, this system would be based in space.

The first satellite early-warning system was called Midas (missile detection and surveillance) and the contract to build it was given to Lockheed in the summer of 1985. They were to construct a satellite with an infrared detecting array that could pick up a massive missile launch by the intense heat of the rocket engines during the burn phase of the launch. Eight of these satellites would be put up in 2,300-mile orbits so that one would be over the Soviet Union at all times.

But Midas didn't work as planned. Even after the second test satellite finally reached orbit (the first blew up), it wasn't working properly. The IR detectors would mistake sunlight reflecting off high-altitude clouds for a missile launch. After a few more test flights, Midas was essentially shelved.

For a time consideration was given to the idea of putting humans in orbit to spot missile launches. Astronauts aboard *Gemini 5* spotted a rocket-sled launch in New Mexico, and the *Gemini 7* astronauts found they could detect submarine-launched Polaris missiles. This was used to bolster the Manned Orbiting Laboratory project. By the time MOL was canceled, however, IR detector technology had improved to the extent that it was ready to test out in space again.

An artist's model of a DSP early-warning satellite. Note how the telescope end of the satellite doesn't point straight down from the satellite, but is angled slightly. [U.S. Air Force]

The new early-warning satellite project eventually became known as the Defense Support Program (DSP). These satellites, which were tested from 1968 until 1971 when they became operational, were placed in geosynchronous orbits. While most geosynchronous satellites follow circular orbits, the DSP satellites were given slight inclinations, 10 degrees or so, so that they would move up and down over the equator. The reason for this is that large parts of the Soviet Union are so far north that they are out of sight from the normal geosynchronous orbit. DSP satellites were designed to be orbited in pairs; while one was above the equator, the other would be below it. The plan called for three sets of these satellites, one over the Indian Ocean to detect Soviet and Chinese missile launches, and two others over the Pacific Ocean and South America to detect submarine launches.

The most interesting feature on a DSP satellite is the 12-foot-long Schmidt telescope. The telescope doesn't point straight down from the satellite but is angled 7.5 degrees. As the satellite is spin-stabilized (kept spinning in orbit to keep it properly aligned, much the same way that a spinning top remains upright), the angled telescope doesn't stare straight down at the Earth's surface, but inscribes a circle, covering a much larger area.

The telescope focuses light onto an array composed of 2,000 IR detectors. The telescope is filtered to admit only light in the near-infrared part of the spectrum, where the emissions of rocket plumes peak. While each detector only covers a 1.5-square mile part of the surface, that is enough for early-warning purposes.

DSP satellites can tell the difference between a blast furnace opening its doors and a rocket launch, because the rocket will move from detector to detector. From that motion it can be determined where the missile is headed, and by calculating the amount of time it was in the burn phase, its impact point can be determined. A DSP satellite can detect a launch within 60 seconds and get a warning to Earth within a minute and a half. Radar stations can then search for the missile and determine when and where the missile will strike, within six minutes.

The DSP satellites now in orbit, however, are vulnerable to blinding by a laser. If a country were to blind a DSP satellite, that would, in itself, be a declaration of war. Another drawback of the DSP satellites is their inability to follow missiles after the burn phase; they become too cool. The goal for the future of IR detection from space is to be able to track a missile along its entire course.

NUCLEAR DETECTION

In the late 1950s, the United States was confident that it could detect Soviet above-ground nuclear weapons tests through a combination of airborne sensors and seismographs. Americans, however, were concerned that as the Soviets ventured into space, they might evade a nuclear test-ban treaty by taking atom bombs behind the Moon and detonating them out of sight. In 1961, TRW received a contract to build satellites that could police a nuclear test ban in outer space by detecting the X-ray, gamma and neutron radiation that nuclear detonations release. The first two of these Vela (Spanish for "watchman") satellites (able to detect nuclear explosions as far away as Venus) were put into 60,000-mile orbits in October 1963, less than three months after the signing of the Nuclear Test Ban Treaty.

The Velas never did detect a nuclear explosion in space (although they did gather useful scientific information on natural radiation phenomena in space). In 1965, after China detonated its first nuclear weapon, it was decided that Vela satellites should also be capable of detecting nuclear blasts on the Earth's surface. The Velas launched from 1967 on were modified to perform that task. The Vela program was canceled in 1970. From then on, nuclear detection sensors were placed aboard the DSP early-warning satellites.

On September 22, 1979, nuclear detection equipment aboard a DSP satellite detected two radiation flashes over Antarctica. The U.S. State Department stated that the flashes were an "indication" of a low-yield, two-kiloton, clandestine nuclear test. South Africa was accused. South African Prime

Minister Pieter Botha denied the allegation, and other radiation tests of the area produced no evidence of such an explosion. Although there has been no completely satisfactory explanation, it has been suggested that the satellite may have been hit by a small meteoroid. These satellites are now equipped with impact sensors that indicate when they've been hit.

There have been plans to refine the nuclear-detection sensors so that they could pinpoint the exact location of a detonation. This would mean that after the first exchange in a nuclear war, the people launching the missiles would know where to send the second barrage, so that the remaining weapons are not wasted on targets that no longer exist. It is ironic that technology originally designed to curb nuclear proliferation would now be included in plans for nuclear war.

ELINT SATELLITES

The intelligence community may be close-mouthed about the photo-reconnaissance satellites, but they are even more secretive about the ELINT—electronic intelligence—gathering satellites.

ELINT gathering targets radio communications, radar signals and missile telemetry. Most ELINT gathering is conducted aboard EC-135 airplanes, huge cargo-type crafts that are jammed with eavesdropping equipment with crews monitoring it that fly along the borders of the Soviet Union and China, occasionally darting over the border to trigger radar alerts. Radar is of particular interest. American and Soviet war planners want to know each other's radar operating frequencies, the speed at which each other's radar antennas rotate and the length of the radar pulses. With such information they can devise electronic countermeasures that would allow bombers to trick and dodge the opponent's radar facilities in time of war. But these planes can't see much beyond the border. Satellites are needed to see what's going on in the heart of the country.

ELINT satellites, also known as *ferrets* for the way they ferret out intelligence, first began orbiting in 1962. Over the next nine years dozens of these satellites in various configurations (some were launched in pairs, some "piggybacked" into space with other payloads, and various orbits were used) were put in orbit.

It seemed strange when the program seemed to come to an end in 1971, for it had been so successful. But of course it hadn't really been terminated. In 1973 and 1977, there were some mysterious launches of military satellites into geosynchronous orbits. They were at first thought to be DSP early-warning satellites. They weren't. In 1977 Americans Christopher Boyce and Andrew Daunton Lee went on trial for selling spy-satellite secrets to the Soviets, revealing the true identity of these mysterious satellites to the world. They were Rhyolites, and they were the new generation of ELINT satellites.

The Rhyolites were designed to monitor Soviet and Chinese missile tests. They are orbited in pairs; one is operational, the other is a backup in case the first one fails. There is one pair over the Horn of Africa to monitor Soviet solid-fuel rocket tests launched from Plesetsk, north of Moscow, and any submarine-launched missiles that pop up out of the White Sea. The other pair hovers over the Indian Ocean, monitoring liquid-fueled launches from Tyuratam in Central Asia, the antiballistic missile test center at Sary Shagan, by Lake Balkash, and the test warhead impacts on the Kamchatka peninsula.

Just as some questioned whether or not the KH-11 alone can meet all of America's satellite-reconnaissance needs, some believe that the *Rhyolite*—renamed Aquacade after the Boyce/Lee affair—isn't enough, especially since President Gerald Ford canceled a successor program, Argus, and the ouster of the shah of Iran in 1979 closed America's best ground-based listening posts. It seems, though that with Rhyolite and the KH-11's ferret capabilities combined,

America's ELINT-gathering needs will be met until a successor to Rhyolite/Aquacade is fully operational.

OCEAN SURVEILLANCE

The U.S. Navy has long wanted to use satellites to spy on the Soviet Navy, but spying on the ocean is harder than spying on land. For one thing, there are no fixed objects; for another, as ships move, intelligence must be virtually real time or it is nearly useless.

The Navy launched its first ocean-surveillance satellite in 1968 and its second in 1971. It is doubtful that either of these satellites were very effective. In 1976 the Navy inaugurated the White Cloud program of passive radar-detecting satellites; they can only detect ships at sea when those ships are using their radar. There is also speculation that White Cloud satellites use IR sensors to try to pick up the slightly warmed water that submarines leave in their wakes.

The Navy's Clipper Bow satellites were to use active radar. They would beam their own radar down to pick up ships crossing the seas and oceans. The technology to do this was out of reach in the 1970s, however, and Clipper Bow was canceled in 1980. It has since been resurrected as ITSS—the Integrated Tactical Surveillance System—which is intended to use radar to track not only ships at sea, but Soviet bombers as well. The technology may still be out of reach.

COMMUNICATIONS AND NAVIGATION

Although not strictly spy satellites, the defense communications and navigation satellites are vital to the military. There are currently several different communications satellite systems in orbit—the general DSCS (defense communications satellite) satellites used by the entire military, as well as the Navy's own FLTSATCOM satellites and the Air Force's AFSATCOM system (which actually operates from other satellites and is used to control the nuclear forces). In time, FLTSATCOM and AFSATCOM will be replaced by a joint system, MILSATCOM, or Milstar.

There are also vital TDRSS—Tracking and Data Relay Satellite System—satellites that are used to relieve vulnerable ground stations around the world of their responsibilities by relaying intelligence through space, directly to the United States. It has been rumored that TDRSS satellites are also used to house various clandestine ELINT-gathering sensors in an attempt to fool the Soviets, who have been known to shut down their radar when identified ELINT satellites go overhead.

The GPS—Global Positioning System, or Navstar—navigation satellites were supposed to be operational in 1987, but the two-and-a-half-year break in the shuttle program after the *Challenger* disaster in 1986 has postponed this. GPS will eventually use 18 satellites in 12,500-mile orbits.

By bouncing signals back and forth between itself and the satellites, any receiving station, whether GPS on the ground or at sea or in the air, will be able to determine its own latitude/longitude position to within 50 feet. This will be useful to ballistic and cruise missiles, which will then be able to guide themselves to their targets with incredible accuracy.

ASATS

In the early 1960s, the great advantage of a spy satellite over a spy plane was that it was invulnerable. It couldn't be knocked out of the sky. In 1968, however, the Soviets began testing their first ASAT—antisatellite weapon. Their system, called FOB (fractional orbital bombardment), employs a hunter-killer satellite that maneuvers alongside the targeted satellite and explodes, destroying itself and its target. Although the Soviet FOB system is essentially operational, it is fairly cumbersome and it takes time to be put in motion. It might take a hunter-killer satellite several orbits before it catches up to its prey.

The United States has taken a different approach, designing the MHV—miniature homing vehicle. The MHV is a direct ascent ASAT in that it is shot into space to hit the target without first going into orbit. The MHV is launched from an airborne F-15 fighter. It is dropped from the fighter and its rocket boosts it quickly to a speed of roughly 40,000 feet per second. The MHV itself is about the size of a basketball and is loaded with sensing equipment, which guides it to its target. It doesn't have any explosives on board and it doesn't need to have any—the impact alone will obliterate both the MHV and the satellite.

American satellite P78-1, a gamma-ray-detecting satellite nearing the end of its operational life, was minding its own business in orbit on September 13, 1985, when its life came to an abrupt and premature end. It was hit in the first successful test of an MHV.

One trouble with ASATs of any kind is that their use in knocking out the enemy's satellites, especially early-warning satellites, would, in itself, amount to a declaration of war. For that reason, they are unlikely to be used except during an all-out nuclear exchange, when both sides would be trying to knock out each other's military satellites.

Efforts have been made to make satellites survivable. One way is to give them enough fuel so that they could evade an ASAT. A more effective approach would be to fit them with electronic countermeasures that they could use to throw off the homing sensors of attacking craft. There are also plans to hide some satellites among the space junk, the old, dead satellites already in orbit, and to fake a satellite's demise, shutting it down as if it were dead, only to bring it back on line in time of emergency.

Finally, there is one truly insidious way of wrecking a satellite that doesn't involve hitting it with anything—"spoofing." The Soviets or the Americans would send signals to the other's satellites, giving them false instructions, pointing them the wrong way, using up their fuel, and sending them into deep space or into the atmosphere. Sophisticated ciphering protects the transmission to and from satellites, but if those codes were broken, there might actually be double agents in space.

9

SOVIET SPY SATELLITES

While the American space program began with much fanfare and stayed in the public eye from the beginning, the Soviet space program was conducted in secrecy. Even Soviet citizens didn't know what was going on. The Soviets provided few figures and no photographs, and when they announced a startling new feat, it seemed to come out of nowhere. There were no personalities. The architect of the program was only referred to, mysteriously, as the "Chief Designer."

The Chief Designer was Sergei Korolev. While Korolev's genius guided the Soviet missile and space program, he himself was victimized repeatedly by the Soviet police state system for much of his life. In the 1930s he was a rising young aeronautics engineer, working with Tupolev, the Soviets' great aircraft designer. Nevertheless, during one of Soviet dictator Josef Stalin's murderous purges, Korolev was imprisoned in a labor camp. He was only allowed out, briefly, after the war, to help examine the captured German V-2 rockets, work that led to the construction of the first all-Soviet rocket, the R-7. Korolev was then sent back to prison and was only released after Stalin died in 1953 and Nikita Khrushchev came to power.

Korolev contributed immensely to the Soviet missile program. But his biggest contribution came in October 1957 when one of his rockets put *Sputnik* into space. From then on Korolev followed each first with another—the first animal in space, first lunar probes, first interplanetary probes, first man in space. But all this time, while Korolev was granted greater liberty under Khrushchev than he had enjoyed under Stalin, he was still kept anonymous. To the world he was only referred to as the Chief Designer, and when he published articles in scientific journals he was only allowed to use the name Sergeyev. He was never allowed to travel outside of the Soviet Union, and when foreign scientists visited Russia, he was not allowed to meet them. The grand architect of the Soviet space program, who died in 1966, was never heralded in his day, even in the Soviet Union, and for most of his adult life he was either in prison or under virtual house arrest.

Korolev was, in part, responsible for one other first that is of particular interest: On April 26, 1962, a Vostok rocket designed by the unsung hero of the Space Age was used to launch the first Soviet reconnaissance satellite, *Cosmos 4.*

When that first Soviet spy satellite went into orbit, no one knew what it was. The Soviets certainly didn't announce it as such. In 1963, amateur satellite trackers, people who listen in on satellites' radio telemetry beeps as they speed across the heavens, noticed something odd about the Soviets' space activities. The Soviets were putting up a greater frequency of satellites and were deorbiting them long before natural orbital decay would have brought them down. And they were releasing even less information on these satellites than they had on previous ones.

One of the amateur satellite trackers following Soviet space activity was Geoffrey E. Perry, a science teacher at the Kettering Grammar School in England. He felt that, given their orbital and launch characteristics, the new Soviet satellites might be military in nature, perhaps flying on reconnaissance missions. Intrigued, he assigned his science class the task of monitoring the Soviet satellites' shortwave radio transmission. It is a class project that has continued for over two decades, and it has produced the bulk of the unclassified information available on the Soviet spy-satellite program. For his work, Perry was awarded an M.B.E.—Member of the Order of the British Empire.

It wasn't just the telemetry that tipped Perry off to the suspicious nature of the new Soviet satellites—it was also where they were launched from. While previous satellites had been launched from the small Kapustin Yar facility, these were sent up from a larger rocket base at Tyuratam in Central Asia. These satellites constituted the first generation of Soviet spy satellites. In terms of the American spy satellite program, these satellites were more like Discoverer than SAMOS in that they returned film to Earth rather than transmitting scanned photos by radio transmission. They were unlike the Discoverer satellites, however, in that the entire satellite, not just a capsule, reentered the atmosphere and it was recovered on the ground, not snatched from the air.

One drawback to the first-generation Soviet spy satellites was that they could only be launched into orbits of 65 degrees inclination or less. They could cover most of the United States that way, but they would miss Alaska and much of the People's Republic of China. To remedy that, the Soviets began launching spy satellites from Plesetsk, a town north of Moscow. These satellites were launched into polar and near-polar orbits. If Tyuratam, with its mix of military and civilian launches, is the Soviet equivalent of Cape Canaveral, then Plesetsk, used solely for polar-orbit military missions, is their Vandenberg.

The second generation of Soviet reconnaissance satellites came in three configurations. There were low-resolution satellites, with resolution on the order of 50 to 80 feet, which made them suitable for broad area surveys and mapping. There were high-resolution satellites that could see things a couple of feet across. Both these satellites only orbited for eight days or so and were not maneuverable in orbit. The third configuration, known to satellite watchers as the extended-duration satellites, could stay in orbit for up to 12 days and were maneuverable.

The third generation of Soviet spy satellites began with a launch in October 1968. Again, there were three types, but this time all enjoyed the extended duration and maneuverability features of the second-generation extended-duration satellites. As before, there were low- and high-resolution satellites, as well as a medium-resolution variety that probably had a resolution on the order of SAMOS (eight feet or so).

The fourth generation is the equivalent of the American Big Bird satellite of the early 1970s, one satellite performing a variety of missions. This generation marked the first time that the entire satellite wasn't deorbited to retrieve the film. As with Big Bird, fourth-generation Soviet spy satellites have recoverable film packs on board that are ejected into the atmosphere. It is believed that this satellite, which first orbited in 1975 but may not have become operational until 1980, may also have some digital-imaging technology on board, not unlike that used by the KH-11, but doubtfully of the same sophistication.

Their equivalent to the KH-11 had its first launch as *Cosmos 1546* on March 29, 1984. Little is known about this satellite. It might not even be operational yet.

Like the United States, the Soviet Union also has an array of military satellites in space on a variety of missions. In 1970 it appeared that a Soviet weather satellite of Meteor class had failed in orbit. When satellites with similar characteristics began to appear, it became apparent that something was up. These satellites have turned out to be Soviet ELINT-gathering craft.

There was some suspicion that the Soviets were employing active SLAR radar in ocean-surveillance satellites in an attempt to monitor ocean traffic. Such satellites would require a large power source to run the radar, perhaps a nuclear generator. This was confirmed in January 1978 when

An artist's concept of a manned Soviet station with a shuttle approaching. The Soviets have already been using their manned station Mir for surveillance tests. Their own shuttle was scheduled for launch in December 1988. [U.S. Air Force]

Cosmos 954 made an uncontrolled reentry into the atmosphere, flinging radioactive debris across the Canadian arctic.

Because much of the Soviet land mass is at high latitudes, out of range of communications satellites on geosynchronous orbit at 22,300 miles above the equator, the Soviets use an eccentric orbit for their communications satellites. Call the Molniya orbit, it has a perigee of only a few hundred miles over the South Pole and an apogee of 25,000 miles or more above the North Pole. When the satellites are high above the Soviet Union they are used to relay communications. By keeping several satellites aloft, communications can be relayed continuously.

In 1972 the Soviets began launching satellites into near-Molniya orbits, but they were not communications satellites, they were early-warning satellites. By using nine of these satellites, evenly spaced, there is always at least one launch-detection satellite high over the United States looking down at it from the north. At that height, it is able to beam any information over the North Pole to command and control centers in the Soviet Union.

The biggest question about the Soviet spy satellites is how they compare to the ones used by the United States. The answer appears to be that while the Soviet spy satellites are not as good as their American counterparts, they have many more of them and have more flexibility.

In terms of sophistication, the Soviets are five or 10 years behind. They only began using their Big Bird after the United States was already using its KH-11, and their KH-11 is just now working as the United States inaugurates the KH-12. This, however, is countered by the fact that the Soviets have many more, cheaper reconnaissance satellites that they can pop into space with only 24-hours' notice. During the Arab-Israeli war of 1973 the Soviets launched seven spy satellites in three weeks.

One question about the Soviet spy satellite program has always been: Why do they bother? It is incredibly easy to gather a great deal of military information openly in the United States. The Soviets have thousands of agents on American soil to gather that which is not so open, the top-secret, classified information.

The Soviets, however, always suspect their enemies of lies and deception, so they, like the United States, need their spy satellites for verification. And the United States is by no means their only intelligence target; the Soviets spy extensively on the Chinese. Further, they will put up a spy satellite in response to any military conflict around the world, just to keep abreast of how other armies are fighting wars.

There is, then, a rough parity between the spy satellite resources of the Soviet Union and the United States. The Soviets have greater flexibility, but the Americans have greater sophistication. Some degree of reassurance can be taken from this, for both sides have a pretty good idea of what the other is up to at all times.

10

THE FUTURE OF OVERHEAD RECONNAISSANCE

AURORA AND THE SPACE SPY PLANE

In May 1988, Secretary of the Air Force Edward C. Aldridge announced that the Air Force would begin to retire the remaining SR-71 spy planes in its inventory. He cited the high cost of operating and maintaining the planes (one flight can cost more than $100,000) and that their mission is duplicated by satellites. What he failed to mention was that there are plans in the works to build an even faster, even higher-flying spy plane.

The Air Force inadvertently revealed a request for $2.1 billion in its 1986 budget request for a project called Aurora, believed to be the code name for the new plane. The contract has been awarded, as usual, to Lockheed, builder of both the U-2 and the SR-71. Undoubtedly, Kelly Johnson, though now aging and ailing, had a hand in Aurora's design.

Estimates are that the plane will be designed to fly at speeds of between Mach 4 and Mach 6 (3,000 to 4,500 mph) and at a height of well over 100,000 feet. Like the SR-71 it will be designed with stealth characteristics—low radar profile, with a radar-absorbing coating—and it will use some type of ramjet engine to power it.

As with the SR-71, one of the main problems with traveling at such speeds is the heat generated: At Mach 6, the temperature on the airplane's outer skin will be 2,500 degrees F. It is likely that new, high-temperature plastics and composite materials will be used to counter the heat. It is also possible that the heat will actually be useful. Flying a plane that high and that fast will require a lot of fuel. There is an exotic but intriguing substance called methylcyclohexane that is useless as fuel at normal temperatures, but at the high temperatures Aurora will reach, it "cracks," or breaks down into toluene and hydrogen, both of which can be used to propel the craft. Aurora will probably fly in the early part of the 1990s.

An artist's concept of an X-30 spaceplane. [U.S. Air Force]

For a spy plane beyond even Aurora, there is the X-30 space plane. Also called a TAV, or Trans-atmospheric Vehicle, the X-30's plans call for it to take off from a runway like a normal plane, then boost up to speeds of up to Mach 25 (17,000 mph or more), achieving an altitude of 100 miles or so, before coming back down. This aero-space plane, as it is also known, was first announced by President Ronald Reagan as a civilian project and was dubbed the Orient Express because it could fly from New York to Peking in 30 minutes.

With the commercial viability of such a project in doubt at the present time (the civil aeronautics industry is more interested in a Mach 3 or 4 plane, not Mach 25), it has become primarily a military venture. If it is ever built, its major value will be as a reconnaissance craft. Part rocket, part plane, it would raise interesting legal issues: Would its use over the Soviet Union constitute a violation of airspace? Estimates are that X-30 will not be ready for its first flight until at least 1994 or 1995. And, in 1995 as today, while the military and intelligence community will show some interest in a high-flying spy plane, the emphasis will still be on the spies in space.

THE KH-12

While the KH-11 was revolutionary, a radical departure from its spy satellite predecessors, the KH-12 was designed to be a new and improved KH-11. It was built with more advanced digital-imaging sensors, as well as ELINT-gathering equipment. They were also designed to provide intelligence even closer to real time than the KH-11. Whereas there were supposed to be two KH-11s in orbit at all times, the mission plan for the KH-12 is to have four in orbit, so that images of any desired target could be relayed to Washington within 20 minutes. To provide such timeliness, flexibility and maneuverability, much of the KH-12's hefty 35,000-pound-plus launch weight is taken up by 15,000 pounds of hydrazine fuel. And when that fuel runs out? No problem, the KH-12 is refuelable.

The notion of a refuelable spy satellite suggests that the space shuttle would be used to carry fuel up into space and pump it into the KH-12's gas tank. Indeed, the shuttle is vital to the KH-12. The new spy satellite was built to fit into the shuttle cargo bay. And as the shuttle carried it into space, no large expendable boosters big enough to carry the KH-12 had to be built. The shuttle, therefore, became the KH-12's only ride into orbit.

In the summer of 1985 there were two KH-11s in orbit, according to plan. The satellites were on overlapping two-year lifetimes; instead of launching two new KH-11s every two years, a new one would be orbited and an old one deorbited every year. In August 1985, the older of the two KH-11s in orbit was brought down from space. Its replacement was set to launch later that month. It never made it into orbit.

THE RECONNAISSANCE CRISIS

As the KH-12 was scheduled to take over in 1986, no more KH-11s were built and the one that blew up was the last KH-11 in inventory. But there was nothing to worry about. Having two KH-11s in orbit was primarily a matter of redundancy; there would be a backup in case one should fail. The KH-11s had been reliable and there was no reason to believe that this one would fail. It had been launched December 4, 1984. By the time it came to the end of its life in late 1986 the KH-12 would be shuttle-launched into orbit.

On January 28, 1986, at 11:38 A.M. EST the *Challenger* space shuttle lifted off from the launchpad 39B at the Kennedy Space Center on Cape Canaveral. Seventy-two seconds after lift-off there was a failure in an O-ring in the joint between two of the sections of one of the solid-rocket boosters. This allowed the burning fuel inside the booster to shoot out of the joint. This spurt of flame cut into the huge adjacent main liquid-fuel tank, detonating it. The tremendous explosion disintegrated the shuttle, killing the seven crew members—mission commander Francis R. Scobee, mission pilot Michael J. Smith, mission specialists Ronald E. McNair, Ellison S. Onizuka and Judith A. Resnik, payload specialist Gregory B. Jarvis and civilian passenger Christa McAuliffe, a schoolteacher from New Hampshire.

The *Challenger* disaster was a national tragedy for America. It was the worst accident in the history of the U.S. space program. It shut down America's manned space program for almost three years. It also drastically curtailed all other unmanned missions. So many American payloads had been designed to be carried into space by the shuttle, and because the shuttle was to be America's primary launch vehicle, no new expendable boosters were being made.

The Air Force had been a little nervous about putting all their eggs in the shuttle basket and had ordered a successor to the old Titans. They ordered 10 of the new Titan 4 boosters (at a cost of $2.09 billion) with the provision that more could be made if necessary. But these new boosters would not be ready in a hurry (not until 1988 as it turned out) and therefore would be no help to the immediate crisis facing the spy satellite program.

This, then, was the situation: There was one KH-11 in orbit that was nearing the end of its operational life. The KH-12 was almost ready to go, but as it was designed for the shuttle and the shuttle was grounded, there was nothing to take it into space until the Titan 4 was ready, which would not be for some time. This meant that there could be a window of vulnerability in 1987 and 1988 when America would be blind from space. Two decisions made in the 1970s had come back to haunt the intelligence community—the decision to make the KH-11 the only spy satellite and the decision to back the shuttle as the primary launch vehicle for military payloads.

Fortunately, there was one last Big Bird in the spy satellite inventory. As well, TRW, the company that built the KH-11, had a test version of the satellite that could be made flight-worthy. So, the Big Bird would be launched into orbit and operated until the demo KH-11 was ready. The Big Bird was launched from Vandenberg at 10:45 A.M. on April 18, 1986. Just under nine seconds after lift-off, when it was 700 feet in the air, the rocket exploded. Debris rained down hard, wrecking sidewalks and cars in the nearby parking lot. The launchpad was crippled. So, it seemed, was America's spy satellite program.

Now, not only was there no shuttle to get the new spy satellite into space, but it also seemed that even the remaining expendable boosters couldn't be trusted.

There was a new plan. While the test version of the KH-11 was readied for flight and while the boosters were checked over, the remaining KH-11 in orbit was put on restricted duty. From then on, in order to conserve fuel, it would only take pictures of high-priority targets. It was estimated that its lifetime could be extended another two years to last into 1988.

On October 26, 1987, one of the remaining old Titan missiles lifted off from Vandenberg with the revamped demo version of the KH-11 aboard. One can imagine that fingers were crossed that day. Fortunately, this launch went without a hitch and the last KH-11 was put into orbit.

As for the future, on September 29, 1988, the space shuttle *Discovery* was launched successfully and America's manned mission to space was back on track. The KH-12 was set to be carried up on the second shuttle flight. One trouble with launching from the shuttle, however, is that shuttles are launched from Cape Canaveral, which means that the KH-12 can't be put directly into a polar orbit.

The answer to this problem was to have been the SLC-6, the Space Launch Complex Six or Slick Six, at Vandenberg. Slick Six was built, at a cost of over $3 billion. But there were problems. The foggy conditions at Vandenberg could postpone many launches. There was also a design flaw: Explosive gases could build up under the launch vehicle, raising the possibility of a terrible disaster. For these and other reasons, Slick Six has now been mothballed. It won't be used at least until 1995, perhaps never. Because of this the KH-12 has been redesigned so that it can be launched by either the space shuttle from Cape Canaveral or the Titan 4 from Vandenberg. If it is shuttle-launched, the KH-12 does have enough fuel to maneuver itself into a polar orbit from

SLC-6, Space Launch Complex Six—or Slick Six—at Vandenberg Air Force Base. Constructed at a cost of more than $3 billion, Slick Six has been mothballed because of design flaws and lack of need. [U.S. Air Force]

the shuttle's orbit. Unmanned spacecraft will be used to refuel it.

Because of the mothballing of Slick Six, and because of fears of the shuttle's reliability, the Air Force's trend for the future will be to get away from the shuttle and put more emphasis on expendable boosters. The Air Force has begun a space recovery program that will last seven years and that is intended to clear up the backlog of spaceflights caused by the shuttle's grounding and the failure of the heavy launch vehicles. The cost of the program is estimated to be $14 billion, which will buy dozens of Titan 4 (the heart of the program), Delta 2, Medium Launch Vehicle-2 and Advanced Launch System boosters and eight of the first 14 shuttle flights after the shuttle program resumes operations. The goal is to gear up to 30 launches per year within five years, tapering off after that to an average of 18 per year.

With the KH-12 in operation, America's spy satellite program is back at full strength. It is intended that the program never be put in jeopardy again.

TEAL RUBY

Highly advanced infrared detection technology is at the heart of much of the future plans for spying from space. The program that employs this has been given the Department of Defense designation *Teal Ruby*. Very simply, a Teal Ruby satellite, if it works as intended, will be the ultimate extension of an early-warning satellite.

Early-warning satellites use infrared detectors to spot rocket engines during their burn phase in a missile launch. The DSP satellites currently performing the early-warning chores have proven themselves to be absolutely reliable by monitoring countless Soviet, Chinese, even American missile tests. The problem with the DSP satellites is that they can only monitor missiles during their burn phase. After that they become too cool for the detectors to follow them for the rest of their flight.

A goal for advanced early-warning satellites, then, would be to follow missiles throughout their ballistic arc. To do this would mean developing advanced IR detectors. An advanced IR-detecting system would have to use active cooling. In the past, the early-warning IR detectors had used the very low temperatures of space—passive cooling—to keep the detectors so cold that they could register the heat given off by missiles thousands of miles away. To pick up a missile after its burn phase, the detectors would have to be cooled even lower. The satellites would have to carry some cryogenic coolant, such as liquid nitrogen, into space with them.

Detector size would also have to be improved. The DSP satellite IR detectors cover 1.5 square miles each. Advanced IR detectors would have to cover a much smaller area if a missile's entire trajectory were to be followed precisely. The key to this is putting as many detector elements on a detector chip as possible. This calls for VLSI—Very Large Scale Integration. The Defense Department wants a chip in which each circuit is only 0.5 microns wide (a micron is one-millionth of an inch). The current state-of-the-art circuit is about five microns across, with some prototypes as small as two and one micron wide. To give an idea of how small 0.5 micron is, the magazine *Aviation Week* figured out that if a map of the United States were to be drawn with lines 0.5 micron wide, every street in the country could be represented in a map only 20 inches wide.

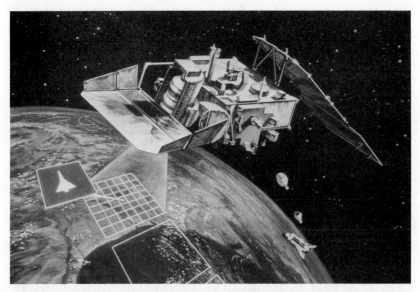

An artist's conception of infrared-detecting satellite Teal Ruby in space, detecting and identifying a plane flying hundreds of miles below. [U.S. Air Force]

Using actively cooled detector arrays, with many, many detector elements crammed into each array, an IR-detection satellite should then be able to track a missile throughout its flight. If that was the case, it was reasoned, why not go a step further? If such a satellite could track relatively cool missiles, it might be able to track airplanes as well. This, then, became the goal: to have a satellite sensing system that could detect and follow anything that moved through the air. This goal gave birth to Teal Ruby.

While DSP satellites orbit at the geosynchronous altitude of 23,000 miles, Teal Ruby satellites were to orbit at 460 miles or so. This would give them much higher resolution, but it would also mean that there would need to be several of the satellites in orbit at any one time to provide complete coverage. The satellite would also be passing swiftly over the surface rather than staring down at it. For this reason the *Teal Ruby* telescope can operate three ways. It can simply stare straight down, letting the surface pass below it; or it can take a broader view, staring ahead toward the horizon; or it can look ahead, lock onto an area, and follow it as it passes below the satellite.

The heart of *Teal Ruby* is its IR-detection capabilities. The sensor elements are made out of mercury cadmium telluride, a substance that is particularly sensitive to emissions in the region of the IR spectrum known as the "blue spike," the point where aircraft-engine emissions peak.

The ultimate goal of Teal Ruby is not only to spot and track aircraft and missiles, but also to identify each and every one of them by their characteristic emissions. To do this the Teal Ruby must work from an extensive data base that will catalogue the emissions of particular aircraft and missiles. There are support programs for Teal Ruby that compile this information as well as information on the background IR clutter (from factory smokestacks, blast furnaces and the like) that Teal Ruby must weed through to find the IR sources it is interested in.

Teal Ruby is now years behind schedule and hundreds of millions of dollars over budget. There were problems with the sensing package, and it was delayed by the grounding of the space shuttle. Although the Teal Ruby program itself may never put an operational satellite system in orbit, its goals will certainly be pursued, even if under a different name.

HALO

Although Teal Ruby will be an exceptionally advanced reconnaissance system, able to track missiles and aircraft in flight, it is, in fact, only the first step to an even more advanced system, HALO (high-altitude large optics).

Planned to begin operation in the mid 1990s, HALO could well be the ultimate spy satellite.

HALO will be revolutionary and the key to its revolutionary aspects is its name. The *high altitude* suggests that HALO may orbit at 22,300 miles, the geosynchronous altitude. Of course, from that distance resolution would be drastically diminished. That's where the large optics come in.

As was mentioned in the section on the KH-11, with adaptive optics that can account for atmospheric distortion, the only thing that limits a satellite's resolution is basically the size of its telescope. The plan for HALO is to build a huge optical system, with focal length measured in meters. One obstacle, however, is the size of the mirror used in the telescope. It is quite expensive to build the big mirrors, and they are very delicate. The answer could well lie in phasar research—phased arrays. Instead of using one large mirror, several smaller ones are used. Phasar work at Kirkland AFB has discovered that a cluster of seven phased telescopes, working in concert to produce one image, results in a resolution that is exponentially greater; seven telescopes don't provide seven times the resolution of one telescope, but 49 times the resolution.

There are great weight penalties in boosting payloads into geosynchronous orbit (the Titan 4 can only lift 10,000 pounds to that height), and so, much work is being done to create a light HALO. There's also the problem of eventually running out of the coolant needed to keep HALO's detectors cold; at most, a two-year supply could be taken up with the satellite. It might be possible to carry replacement fuel into a lower orbit aboard the shuttle, then ferry it out to the HALO satellite by interorbital tug.

The advantages of having a spy satellite in geosynchronous orbit more than compensate for the problems and costs. While both the KH-11 and the KH-12 provide near-real-time intelligence, they fly over the Earth's surface. The HALO satellites (there will be several, spaced out along the geosynchronous orbits) will be staring down at the planet surface, able to point their telescopes wherever they wish—at troop deployments here, a shipyard there—and be able to beam down true real-time intelligence.

An artist's concept of a HALO satellite. Orbiting at very high geosynchronous altitude, HALO satellites would have to be constructed out of very thin, light-weight materials. [U.S. Air Force]

And there will be improvement in how the intelligence is processed. High-speed computers, using principles of artificial intelligence, will do much of the preliminary work of photo interpreters, figuring out what it is that the satellite sees. HALO will also satisfy the military commanders, providing tactical intelligence. The TENCAP—Tactical Exploitation of National Capabilities—program is supposed to create mobile receiving units, so that a commander will be able to tap into HALO (or, until HALO is ready, other spy satellites) and see what the enemy is doing 20, 30, 100 miles away.

A shuttle-launched test of HALO, using a mini-version at a lower altitude, was scheduled to be orbited in 1988. With the shuttle grounding, that has been postponed several years. Considering that and the fact that most programs take longer than planned, HALO will not likely be operational until sometime toward the end of the century. While in most respects HALO would be the ultimate spy satellite, there are some people who continue to insist that the ultimate spy in space must be a man.

THE SPACE STATION

NASA has always looked for big projects to keep it busy. After the Apollo program fulfilled its goal and landing men on the Moon became run-of-the-mill, NASA came up with the idea of the space shuttle to send payloads into space with a reusable launch vehicle. The shuttle was fully operational before the *Challenger* disaster, being used to launch dozens of satellites, repair a couple of satellites in space that were disabled and bring another back to Earth for repair. Although the nearly three-year layoff after *Challenger* threw a wrench into the works, it shouldn't be long before the shuttle is back on a regular mission schedule. In preparation for the future, NASA has been looking ahead to its next big project—the space station.

What NASA has in mind is not the huge spinning wheel under construction in Stanley Kubrick's movie *2001: A Space Odyssey* but a much more modest station, with a cylindrical hub that would house four to six people and attached minifactories and ports where shuttles and interorbital tugs could dock. It would be modular in design to allow adding onto. It would be vital to any further manned exploration of space; the kind of huge spacecraft needed to get men to Mars, for example, would be too big to launch all in one piece from the Earth's surface and would have to be assembled in space.

But in this era of budget consciousness it would be necessary for the space station to make commercial sense. The microgravity environment could be used to make exceptionally pure medicines, better silicon chips for computers and perfectly round ball bearings. With a start-up cost of $9 billion or more and an overall cost of at least $30 billion, however, it is unlikely that the space station would be able to pay for itself making perfectly round ball bearings.

Undoubtedly the space station's biggest customer would be the military. At least that's what NASA is counting on, just as it counted on the military to be the space shuttle's biggest customer. Such huge projects are simply no longer viable without the military's involvement. The question is whether or not the military wants to get involved.

NASA has touted to the military the value of manned reconnaissance in space. This is basically the same thing as MOL—the Manned Orbiting Laboratory—of 10 years before. The same arguments apply as they did then: A man in space could be used to aim reconnaissance equipment and repair it if necessary. On the other hand, it's still incredibly costly to get men into space, and, given the success of the unmanned reconnaissance satellites, is it worth it? Dr. Robert S. Cooper, the director of the Defense Advanced Research Projects Agency (the agency behind HALO and Teal Ruby), stated in 1983, before the Subcommittee on Defense of the House Appropriations Committee, that "In ten years of groping, we haven't figured out how to use a man in space. We think it's a good idea, but we aren't sure why."

To find out why it might be a good idea, the military will be conducting 11 exercises aboard the eight shuttle flights it has scheduled out of the first 14 after the program resumes. All of these exercises, in one way or another, have something to do with surveillance and reconnaissance. These exercises will be coordinated with ground tests—missile firings, troop movements and the like. The USAF Spaceborne Direct View System is one of the major systems to be tested in an exercise. It will be used to see how well strategic reconnaissance— looking at missile bases and shipyards—can be performed by men in space. Exercise Army Terra Scout will test battlefield reconnaissance capabilities, and Army Terra Geode will test the ability to scout rough terrain—both with hand-held viewing systems. There will also be exercises to see how well men can spot missile launches, pick up ships at sea, watch Soviet activities in space and spot and track targets.

NASA does not yet have the military's full backing for the space station. It doesn't help that the station will, in part, be a joint venture with Canada and other nations. An agreement was signed on September 29, 1988, the day the shuttle resumed flight. This scares the military for security reasons (conversely, potential American military involvement annoys the other nations). Nevertheless, the military is interested, perhaps because the Soviets have their own space station, the Mir, and they have been testing out the idea of flesh-and-blood spies in space themselves. The American military does not want to be left behind.

Even if the military does not get wholeheartedly involved in the manned space station, there is the possibility that they may build an *unmanned* space station of their own. There is great interest in the field of artificial intelligence (AI) in the military. Computers with AI capabilities would almost be able to think for themselves; they would be able to mimic the human mind to a degree. Instead of sending men into space, machines could be sent that could perform the tasks of spotting targets, pointing reconnaissance systems and even making repairs. Every now and then, unmanned spacecraft might dock with the station to refuel it.

An unmanned space station, as far as the military is concerned, would have most of the benefits of a manned space station with a lower cost and no risk of the loss of human life. There may be plans for such a station in the works right now. If there are, this new space-based reconnaissance platform may have already been given its designation. It may be the KH-13.

11

HOW SPY SATELLITES ARE USED

In the middle of an industrial park in Sunnyvale, California, a town south of San Francisco, there stands a pale blue windowless building, known, appropriately enough, as the Big Blue Cube. This is the Satellite Test Center (STC), headquarters for the Satellite Control Facility (SCF). The SCF comprises a network of eight satellite ground stations around the world, including the STC. The Big Blue Cube is master control for America's fleet of military satellites, including the KH-11.

The satellites are controlled by the STC via ground stations around the world. If a command has to be sent to the KH-11 as it passes up over the Atlantic toward the North Pole, the STC would issue the command to the ground station in Thule, Greenland, which would, in turn, communicate to the satellite. Because the Big Blue Cube is vulnerable to a terrorist or nuclear attack, there is a backup STC ready go to on line at a moment's notice that is built into the underground Consolidated Space Operations Center near Colorado Springs, Colorado.

Information from the KH-11 is beamed down to the continental United States at Fort Belvoir, Virginia. The digital imagery is then directed to NPIC (the National Photographic Interpretation Center), another windowless building located at the corner of M Street and First Street, eight blocks from the Capitol building in Washington, D.C. Although

NPIC was, at one time, the premier photo interpretation unit in the nation, the fact that both the CIA and the Defense Intelligence Agency have their own interpretation units suggests that NPIC may really have become more of an image storage bank than an interpretation center.

Once the images gathered by the KH-11 are in Washington and hard copies have been made, they are distributed to the people with the appropriate clearance in the intelligence community who requested them.

The clearance hierarchy is governed by the policy of Security Compartmented Information. This is also known as the "need to know" policy; you only get to see what you have to see. There are three types of clearance. An SI (Special Intelligence) clearance allows you access primarily to ELINT gathered from satellites. A TK (Talent Keyhole—Talent is the code name for spy plane-gathered intelligence; Keyhole denotes satellite-gathered intelligence) clearance allows you access to all overhead reconnaissance imagery. A Byeman clearance lets you in on the operational information concerning the spy equipment used; you'd get to peruse the KH-11 manual, for example.

The organization responsible for running the spy satellites is the National Reconnaissance Office (NRO), the agency that launches the satellites and operates them in space. The NRO does not officially exist. Its cover within the Pentagon is the Office of Space Systems.

This generally unheard-of, hidden office of Air Force Intelligence is the single largest member of the intelligence community, five or six times the size of the CIA in terms of budget and manpower. It has over 50,000 employees. As for budget (estimated, as it doesn't officially have a budget), it currently operates on about $4 billion a year. The total tab for running the spy satellites in the 1980s, tallying up all the money kicked in by the CIA, the National Security Agency, the Navy and others, will be in excess of $50 billion—more than twice what it cost to put men on the Moon, even with inflation.

As mentioned, President Eisenhower created the NRO to coordinate all spy-satellite activities and stop the war for control between the CIA and the Air Force. To make it civilian and to divide the power between the two, he set it up so that the head of the NRO would be the undersecretary of the Air Force and the second in command would come from the CIA. This did not smooth everything over between the Air Force and the CIA. The CIA has built the last two satellites—the KH-11 and KH-12—much to the chagrin of the Air Force, which wanted a variety of smaller satellites.

The NRO is overseen executively by the National Reconnaissance Executive Committee (NREC), which is chaired by the Director of Central Intelligence (DCI), the head of the CIA, with representatives from the Department of Defense. NREC reports to the secretary of defense.

While the NRO operates the spy satellites, it does not, itself, decide what pictures the satellites are going to take. That is the job of COMIREX—the Committee on Overhead Imagery Requirements and Exploitation, which is itself a subcommittee of NFIB—the National Foreign Intelligence Board. NFIB is chaired by the DCI, with voting representatives from the various members of the intelligence community—the NRO, the CIA, the NSA, the State Department, the FBI and the Department of Energy and the Treasury—and nonvoting representatives from the armed service intelligence agencies (Army, Navy, Marines and Air Force). Requests for images are made to COMIREX and, generally at the recommendation of COMIREX, are granted or denied by NFIB.

If all that seems like an overly complicated and involved bureaucracy, that's because it is—and that's the way it was intended. For one thing, the satellites can only take so many images and there are many more requests denied than granted. For another, the bureaucracy is set up with checks, balances and overlapping responsibilities so that no one agency can dominate the use of the satellites. The CIA and the military are still at loggerheads over what kind of intelligence to gather. The CIA wants strategic information (intelligence on the long-term plans and capabilities of the enemy); the military wants tactical intelligence (intelligence on the enemy's immediate military positions and plans); and the bureaucracy keeps their influence balanced fairly evenly.

What the bureaucracy cannot prevent is the ultimate political use of the intelligence gathered. One tends to think of intelligence, especially hard and fast intelligence such as reconnaissance photos, as almost apolitical. Intelligence gathering is *supposed* to be apolitical, but it has never quite worked that way; the Army might use one piece of intelligence to support its request for a new weapons system, while the CIA might contradict that piece of intelligence with its own, perhaps after some encouragement from a budget-minded president.

Until 1972, the political use of intelligence was kept, for the most part, behind closed doors and out of the public eye. In 1972, however, the United States signed the SALT I—Strategic Arms Limitation Talks—agreement with the Soviet Union to rein in the arms race. Article V of that agreement states, in part, that "...each party shall use national technical means of verification at its disposal" to verify the treaty. These "national technical means" were none other than the spy satellites in use by both countries.

It wasn't until 1978, though, that the spy satellites became a truly public political issue. The administration of President Jimmy Carter had negotiated with the Soviets on a SALT II treaty. Conservatives and skeptics in the United States were afraid that the Soviets would cheat on the treaty. Carter became the first president in history to refer directly to the reconnaissance satellites and their abilities. He was a believer. Indeed, on the day of his inauguration in January 1977, the KH-11 sent down its first pictures and Carter was given a look. He was impressed. But in arguing his case, he could not actually show the public what the satellites could do, and there were other "experts" to disagree with him. The SALT II treaty was never ratified by the U.S. Senate.

The question of the spy satellites' ability to verify an arms treaty remains a contentious political issue to this day. Generally, those who support arms control think that the satellites are up to the job, and those who do not support arms control think they are inadequate. Who's right?

Those opposed to arms control cite several instances where the Soviets have violated SALT II, which although never signed by the United States has, by agreement, been followed by both countries. The question is, how did the United States ever find out that the Soviets had violated SALT II if the satellites couldn't tell either way?

Would it be possible for the Soviets to cheat on an arms agreement? Yes, they could, but not to any significant degree according to arms control supporters. You can't hide the construction of a new missile system, or bomber or submarine; the KH-11 can see at night and through clouds. Even if the Soviets tried to build something on a huge scale underground, there would be so many other clues, such as what was going in and out of the complex, for one, that the end result would be the same.

Arms-control opponents, however, point to the Soviet construction of a huge antiballistic missile radar base at Abalakova in Siberia. According to them, this large base (which if operational would contravene the antiballistic missile agreement signed in the early 1970s) went undetected by spy satellites for over a year. This isn't the case. In truth, the KH-11 did detect the construction of the radar base right from the beginning, it was just that no one knew exactly what it was for a year. It was still identified, after one of the last close-look satellites in the inventory was sent up to take pictures, long before it became operational. The Americans protested the construction of the base and the Soviets have halted completing it.

One thing that probably does stymie the KH-11 in terms of treaty verification is the MIRV—the multiple impact reentry vehicle. These are missiles with several different warheads under one nose cone, each independently targeted. Arms-control opponents would argue that the KH-11 can't see how many warheads a MIRV nose cone contains. They may or may not be right. Even if they are right, the simple solution, in terms of treaty negotiation and verification, is to assume that every MIRV spotted has the maximum number of warheads that such a vehicle can hold, until proven otherwise.

As President Carter discovered, however, it isn't possible to demonstrate to the public what spy satellites can do. This is because they are shrouded in such intense secrecy. What is interesting here is that surely the Soviets know all they need to know about the spy satellites; they bought a manual for the KH-11 from former CIA employee William Kampiles, and Christopher Boyce and Daunton Lee sold them secrets about the Rhyolite ELINT satellites. This means that the only people who don't know about the spy satellites are the public.

This isn't because the intelligence community wants to keep the information from the public. It's just that they are not entirely sure what it is that the Soviets know, and they don't want any publicly released information to provide the Soviets with that one small piece of the puzzle that they were looking for. In fact, the intelligence community isn't all that fond of books like the one you are now reading. They don't like writers guessing about the spy satellites in case they happen to guess right.

As it happens, the veil of secrecy is slowly beginning to lift from the spy satellite program, no thanks to the American intelligence community. The secrecy is evaporating slightly because now the public can buy its own spy satellite photos. The French have an imaging satellite, the *SPOT—Systeme Probatoire d'Observation de la Terre*—that produces pictures with a ground resolution of about 30 feet. The public can buy these photos (if they aren't in *SPOT*'s inventory they can be ordered) for a price ranging from a few hundred dollars to a few thousand. Not to be left out of the commercial market, the Soviets plan to sell photos from a lower-resolution satellite around the world through an agency called Soyuzkarta. This program suffered a setback in January 1988 when the satellite taking the pictures malfunctioned and the Soviets destroyed it (instead of letting it fall to Earth and possibly into American hands).

While the *SPOT* satellite is not nearly as sophisticated as the American and Soviet spy satellites, the two superpowers are no longer the only ones to possess high-quality military reconnaissance satellites. In 1975 China began sending up its own 10,000-pound reconnaissance satellites from the Shuang-Cheng-Tzu Space Center, 1,000 miles west of Peking. On September 19, 1988, Israel launched its first satellite, the *Horizon 1*, into orbit. Although it was hotly denied by Israeli officials that *Horizon* is a spy satellite, it is probably the first step towards building a spy satellite program that some estimate will cost Israel $10 billion. Israel wants its own spy satellites so it can monitor the growing proliferation of ballistic missiles in the Middle East, and because it no longer wants to have to depend on the United States for reconnaissance information.

The United States and the Soviet Union were first, but now other countries have lept into space in an attempt to seize the high observational ground. Others are sure to follow, for, if a country can afford it, the prospect of knowing—really knowing—what the other side is up to is just too tantalizing to resist.

Several times in this book the ironical nature of the spy-satellite program has been mentioned; that spy satellites were only made possible because of the development of missiles, which are, in fact, the primary reconnaissance targets of the satellites. In recent years a further twist to the irony has been added—the SDI—Strategic Defense Initiative—or "Star Wars" plan put forward by President Reagan in March 1983. The original concept of SDI called for space- and land-based laser or particle beam stations that, in the event of a nuclear attack, would blast incoming Soviet missiles out of the sky.

The plan, which was originally estimated to cost $1 *trillion* over the next 20 years, has since been scaled back because of fiscal restraint and technological reality. The idea now is not to stop all the missiles (which would be impossible), but to block such a high percentage that Soviet war planners would think twice about launching a surprise attack. Opponents of the plan argue that it is destabilizing; that the Soviets, fearing that the United States might use SDI as a shield from behind which to launch its own first strike, might be more inclined, in time of crisis, to launch a preemptive first strike before the SDI shield is operational.

Those arguments aside, one interesting thing about SDI is how the plan involves spy satellites. A crucial—if not *the* crucial—part of the plan is the spotting, tracking and targeting of the incoming missiles. That is a task that would be most suited to Teal Ruby and HALO-type spy satellites.

Initially spy satellites were built in an effort to lessen ultimately the chance of war. When both sides know what the other is doing and know that each other knows, war is less likely. With treaty verification duties, that role for spy satellites became entrenched. Now, however, the satellites are to be included in the war plans themselves.

Somehow, this completes the circle. When the first overhead reconnaissance began it was all conducted for the military. It was only with the CIA's development and operation of the spy planes and spy satellites in the 1950s that overhead reconnaissance, at least in the United States, became a civilian program. Now with the SDI plans for the future, we come full circle and the spy-in-the-sky is back in uniform.

GLOSSARY

AFB
Air Force base.

AFSATCOM
Air Force satellite communications.

Aquacade
ELINT-gathering spy satellite.

ASAT
antisatellite weapon.

Aurora
American spy plane proposed to replace the SR-71.

Big Bird
A combined area-survey/close-look spy satellite.

BMEWS
ballistic missile early warning system.

Byeman
Clearance for information regarding the operations of spy satellites and spy planes.

CIA
Central Intelligence Agency.

Clipper Bow
Defunct Navy active radar satellite program.

COMIREX	Committee on Overhead Imagery Requirements and Exploitation.
DEW	distant early warning.
Discoverer	American recoverable-capsule spy-satellite program.
DoD	Department of Defense.
DSCS	Defense communications satellite.
DSP	Defense Support Program.
ELINT	Electronic intelligence.
FLTSATCOM	Fleet satellite communications.
FOB	fractional orbital bombardment.
GPS	Global Positioning System.
HALO	High-altitude large optics.
HUMINT	Human intelligence, or intelligence gathered by people.
ICBM	Intercontinental ballistic missile.
IR	Infrared.
IRBM	Intermediate range ballistic missile.
ITSS	Integrated Tactical Surveillance System.

KH-1	Keyhole designation for SAMOS satellites.
KH-2	Keyhole designation for Discoverer satellites.
KH-5	Second generation of area-survey satellites.
KH-6	Second generation of close-look satellites.
KH-7	Third generation of area-survey satellites.
KH-8	Third generation of close-look satellites.
KH-9	Keyhole designation for Big Bird.
KH-10	Keyhole designation for defunct Manned Orbiting Laboratory.
KH-11	America's first digital imaging spy satellite.
KH-12	Newest generation of American digital imaging spy satellite.
M-4	A Soviet bomber.
Midas	Missile detection and surveillance.
MiG	Soviet fighter plane.

MILSATCOM	Military satellite communications.
Milstar	Same as MILSATCOM.
M.I.T.	Massachusetts Institute of Technology.
MIRV	Multiple impact reentry vehicle.
MHV	Miniature homing vehicle.
MOL	Manned Orbiting Laboratory.
MRBM	Medium-range ballistic missile.
NACA	National Advisory Committee for Aeronautics.
NASA	National Aeronautics and Space Administration.
NFIB	National Foreign Intelligence Board.
NPIC	National Photographic Interpretation Center.
NREC	National Reconnaissance Executive Committee.
NRO	National Reconnaissance Office.
NSA	National Security Agency.
OBC	Optical bar camera.

O.S.S.	Office of Strategic Services.
PHOTINT	Photographic intelligence.
PI	Photo interpreter.
RAF	Royal Air Force.
RAND	Research and Development Corporation.
RB-47	Bomber turned reconnaissance plane.
RC-135	Cargo plane turned ELINT-gathering spy plane.
RF-86	Sabrejet fighter turned reconnaissance plane.
RF-101	Voodoo fighter turned reconnaissance plane.
Rhyolite	ELINT-gathering spy satellite program.
RPV	Remotely piloted vehicle.
RSO	Reconnaissance systems operator.
SAC	Strategic Air Command.
SALT	Strategic Arms Limitation Talks.
SAM	Surface-to-air missile.

SAMOS	Satellite and Missile Observation System.
SCF	Satellite Control Facility.
SDI	Strategic Defense Initiative.
SI	Special Intelligence—clearance for satellite-gathered ELINT.
SLAR	Side-looking airborne radar.
SLGS	Space-link ground system.
SR-71	American spy plane.
STC	Satellite Test Center.
Teal Ruby	Infrared detection and tracking satellite program.
TENCAP	Tactical Exploitation of National Capabilities.
TDRSS	Tracking and Data Relay Satellite System.
TIROS	Television and Infrared Observation System.
TK	Talent Keyhole—clearance for all overhead reconnaissance intelligence.
U-2	American spy plane.

U.S.S.R.   Union of Soviet Socialist
                       Republics.

V-1   World War II German buzz
                       bomb; cruise missile.

V-2   World War II German ballistic
                       missile.

Vela   Defunct nuclear radiation detec-
                       tion satellite program.

White Cloud   Navy passive radar-detection
                       satellite program.

WS-117L   First designation of spy satellite
                       program.

X-30   Proposed American space plane.

SUGGESTED READING

Ambrose, Stephen E., with Immerman, Richard H. *Ike's Spies: Eisenhower and the Espionage Establishment*. New York: Doubleday and Co., 1981.

Burrows, William E. *Deep Black*. New York: Random House, 1986.

Cline, Ray S. *Secrets, Spies and Scholars: Blueprint of the Essential CIA*. Washington, D.C.: Acropolis Books, 1976.

Karas, Thomas. *The New High Ground: Systems and Weapons of Space Age War*. New York: Simon & Schuster, 1983.

Klass, Phillip J. *Secret Sentries in Space*. New York: Random House, 1971.

Lindsey, Robert. *The Falcon and the Snowman*. New York: Pocket Books, 1980.

Marchetti, Victor, and Marks, John D. *The CIA and the Cult of Intelligence*. New York: Laurel Books, 1980.

Oberg, James. *Red Star in Orbit*. New York: Random House, 1981.

Powers, Gary, with Gentry, Curt. *Operation Overflight*. New York: Holt, Rinehart and Winston, 1970.

Talbott, Strobe. *Endgame: The Inside Story of Salt II*. New York: Harper Colophon Books, 1980.

Wolfe, Tom. *The Right Stuff*. New York: Farrar, Straus and Giroux, 1979.

Yost, Graham. *Spy-Tech*. New York: Facts On File, 1985.

INDEX

C

C-119 (U.S. cargo plane) 75-77
CARTER, Jimmy (James Earl Carter Jr.)
138, 140
CASTRO Ruz, Gen. Fidel
Cuban Missile Crisis 39-46
CBS Laboratories 67
CENTRAL Intelligence Agency (CIA) ix
Cuban Missile Crisis 41-46
Discoverer Spy Satellite Program 59-84
Intelligence Budget 136
KH-11 98, 100
Manned Orbiting Laboratory (MOL)
91-93
SAMOS Spy Satellite Program xii,
77-85, 94
Satellite Use 136
SR-71 Blackbird 48-58
U-2 Incident 38
U-2 Program 13-30
CHALLENGER (U.S. space shuttle) 109,
122-125, 131
CHINA, People's Republic of
Nuclear Detection 105-107
Reconnaissance xi, 141
SR-71 Blackbird 47, 55
CHINA, Republic of (Taiwan) 47
CIA—See CENTRAL Intelligence Agency
CIVIL War, U.S. (1861-65) 2, 14
CL-400 (U.S. spy plane) 48
CLARKE, Arthur C. 63
CLINE, Ray 21, 44, 73
CLIPPER Bow (U.S. radar satellite program) 108
CLOSE-Look Satellites—See KH-6
COMIREX—See OVERHEAD Imagery Requirements and Exploitation
COMMUNICATIONS Satellites 108-109;
illus. 71
CONSOLIDATED Space Operations Center 135
COOPER, Gordon 89
COOPER, Robert S. 132
CORONA Project 69
COSMOS 4 (Soviet reconnaissance satellite) 114
COSMOS 954 (Soviet reconnaissance satellite) 117
COSMOS 1546 (Soviet reconnaissance satellite) 116
COTTON, Sidney 6-7, 10
CRATOLOGY 40
CUBA, Republic of
Missile Crisis 7, 39-46
CUBAN Missile Crisis 7, 39-46

D

D-21 Drone 55
DEEP Black (book) 81
DEFENSE, U.S. Department of
Military Satellite Programs 101
Recoverable Satellites 69
Teal Ruby Satellite Program 126-128
DEFENSE Advanced Research Projects
Agency 132
DEFENSE Communications Satellite
(DSCS) 108
DEFENSE Intelligence Agency (DIA)
Cuban Missile Crisis 41
Satellite Use 136
DEFENSE Support Program (DSP) 103-105, 126; illus. 103
De GAULLE, Gen. Charles Andre Joseph
Marie (1890-1970) 37, 82
DEW Line—See DISTANT Early Warning
Line
DIA—See DEFENSE Intelligence Agency
DIRIGIBLES 4
DISCOVERER (U.S. spy satellite program) 59-85, 94, 115; illus. 75
DISCOVERER 1 (U.S. spy satellite) 72
DISCOVERER 2 (U.S. spy satellite) 72
DISCOVERER 11 (U.S. spy satellite) 73
DISCOVERER 12 (U.S. spy satellite) 73
DISCOVERER 13 (U.S. spy satellite) 75;
illus. 74, 76
DISCOVERER 14 (U.S. spy satellite) 77,
79, 79; illus. 78
DISCOVERER 15 (U.S. spy satellite) 79
DISCOVERER 16 (U.S. spy satellite) 80
DISCOVERER 17 (U.S. spy satellite) 80
DISCOVERER 18 (U.S. spy satellite) 80
DISCOVERER 31 (U.S. spy satellite) 83
DISCOVERY (U.S. space shuttle) 124
DISTANT Early Warning (DEW) Line 15,
101; illus. 102
DSCS—See DEFENSE Communications
Satellite
DSP—See DEFENSE Support Program
DULLES, Allen W(elsh) (1893-1969) 17-19, 28, 73

E

EARLY-Warning Satellites 101-105, 117
EASTMAN Kodak Co. 7, 58, 67
EC-135 (U.S. reconnaissance plane) 106
EISENHOWER, Dwight David (Ike) (1890-1969)
Discoverer Spy Satellite Program 73,
77